WHITE DWARF

MAY 2018

THE RULERS BENEATH THE WAVES

Over the past few weeks, you can't have failed to notice the Idoneth Deepkin emerging into the world. This month, following on from last month's preview and Ultimate Guide feature, we dive deeper with a look at all the new kits in Planet Warhammer and the lowdown on their design and the inspiration behind them in Designers' Notes and Paint Splatter painting guides for the Namarti Thralls and Akhelian King. You can see the army in action in our Battle Report, fought out over the amazing Realm of Death board we featured in last month's Battleground, no less!

On top of all that, in what we think is one of the highlights of the issue, we've got a brand-new 'Eavy Metal Masterclass, from the team's Martin Peterson. Check it out over on page 36. And for more top-notch painting, we've got something a little special in Golden Demon this month – the inaugural White Dwarf Golden Demon Winners' Challenge. You can find it on page 48.

Elsewhere in a typically packed issue, we've got new rules for Necromunda – Gangs of Bounty Hunters working together! – and a painting guide for the new Doom Lords Blood Bowl team. There's also a brilliant minigame – Duels of the Crystal Labyrinth – pitting Tzeentch's sorcerers against one another on page 100, and so much more. Enjoy!

Matt K

WHAT IS WHITE DWARF?

White Dwarf is the ultimate Warhammer magazine. For more than 40 years, it has been the essential guide to everything going on with Citadel Miniatures and the Games Workshop hobby, bringing you an in-depth look at the latest games and miniatures, Battle Reports, painting guides, modelling tips and more. White Dwarf is 148 pages of the very best the hobby has to offer, each and every month.

We have a saying in the White Dwarf office: "Every issue is somebody's first." If you are a newer reader or you've been away for a while, check out the 'Start Here' section over the page (you can find it over on the right) for some suggestions on where you might like to start with this issue and where to find more information. And for more about White Dwarf, find us on Facebook: 'White Dwarf Magazine'.

CONTENTS

58 Two T'au armies. Two Space Marine armies. One seriously messy Blitz mission!

72 Can Nagash and his undead legion stop the Idoneth Deepkin from stealing souls?

108 Even Bounty Hunters need mates sometimes. This time they form their own gang!

40 From Ryza they came, an Adeptus Mechanicus battle congregation painted by Jason Lee.

28 We chat to Seb Perbet and Ben Jefferson about designing the new Idoneth Deepkin.

START HERE

New to White Dwarf or just new to the issue? Here's our picks for some great places to start this month.

If you're new to our games and worlds, you can find out more about all of our key games and brands in the White Dwarf Guide on page 136.

PLANET WARHAMMER

ALL THE LATEST NEWS ABOUT THE GAMES WORKSHOP HOBBY!

IDONETH DEEPKIN

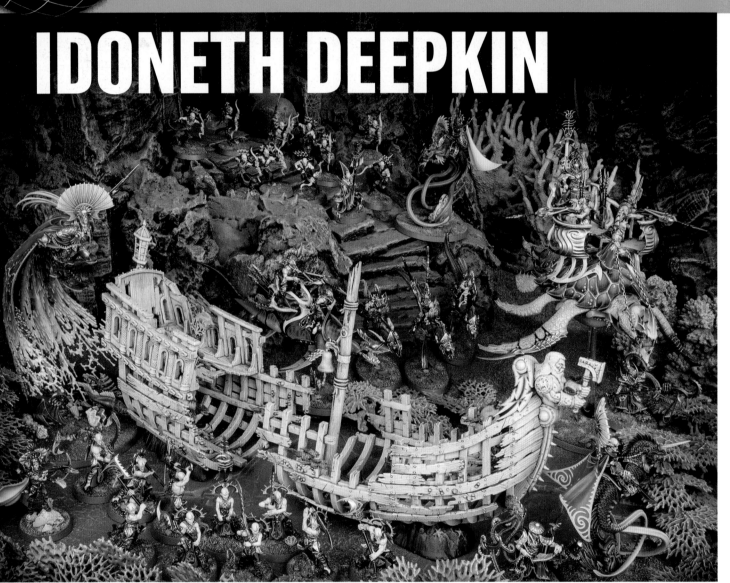

This month in Planet Warhammer, we've got lots to talk about, so grab a cup of tea and a tasty biscuit, sit back and enjoy the journey as we take a look at two new codexes, new models from our specialist games range, new scenery, paints and brushes, a war machine for the Horus Heresy and, of course, the full Idoneth Deepkin range.

The Idoneth Deepkin are a new faction for Warhammer Age of Sigmar – you may well have read the Ultimate Guide for them in last month's issue and seen some of them on the Warhammer Community site. This month, all the kits for the Idoneth are out – you can see them over the following pages. You can also find out more about how they were designed in Designers' Notes on page 28, see them in action on the battlefield in our Battle Report on page 72 and learn how to paint them in Paint Splatter on page 120.

PLENTY OF FISH IN THE SEA

This issue features loads of content about the Idoneth Deepkin. First, you can find out about the new models in Planet Warhammer (that's this bit). Then on page 28 we've got Designers' Notes on the new range of miniatures, followed by a Battle Report on page 72 where they take on the Legions of Nagash in the Realm of Death. Then, to round things off, on page 120 you can find Paint Splatter, which features stage-by-stage guides for the Akhelian King and a Namarti Thrall in the colours of the Ionrach Enclave. That should keep you busy!

Also out this month are two new codexes, one for the Deathwatch, the other for the Harlequins. Codex: Deathwatch now includes rules for Primaris Space Marine Kill Teams and characters such as the Apothecary, while Codex: Harlequins features not only rules for Harlequins, but rules for a brand-new scenery piece, too – the Aeldari Webway Gate, which you can see on page 11. The Webway gate is not the only piece of scenery out this month – the Gloomtide Shipwreck is also available – a great piece of scenery for any battle taking place in the Mortal Realms.

This month we also take a look at two new paints for the Idoneth Deepkin (we use them in Paint Splatter), the Van Saar gang for Necromunda, the Doom Lords Chaos Chosen team for Blood Bowl (both have lots of extras available to them) and the Termite assault transport. Let's hope that cup of tea is big enough, eh?

THE NAMARTI CORPS

When the Idoneth go to war, it's the soul-cursed Namarti that form the first attack wave. Though blind from birth, they can sense the movements of their foes in the ethersea around them, enabling them to bring their deadly weapons to bear.

There are two plastic sets for the Namarti – one containing 10 Namarti Thralls the other 10 Namarti Reavers. The Namarti Thralls kit contains seven male and three female aelves with an array of deadly Lanmari blades, from razor-edged glaives and falchions to arrow-headed halberds. The Namarti Thralls are easily recognised by the barbed iron collars they wear around their necks and the scalloped greaves on their lower legs (and their massive blades, of course). The sprue also includes six base details such as a clam and a stalk of coral. The Namarti Reavers carry keening blades and whisperbows which, like all Namarti weapons, are engraved with the half-soul rune. The Namarti Reavers are sculpted running forward while firing their bows, using their preternatural sense to track their prey. There are four female and six male aelves in this set and the heads are interchangeable with those in the Thralls kit.

FIVE THINGS WE LOVE IN... MAY

5 Warhammer Fest! It's the biggest event of the Games Workshop calendar and it takes place on 12 and 13 May. There may still be tickets left for the event, which is promising to be the biggest we've ever run. You can find out more and order tickets here: warhammerworld.games-workshop.com

4 New rules for Harlequins and Deathwatch. Both factions now have new codexes, complete with warlord traits, stratagems and relics. The Great Harlequin stratagem proved especially interesting to us, while the Mission Tactics for the Deathwatch look particularly deadly.

IDONETH DEEPKIN NAMARTI REAVERS

Available: Now

£30, €40, 300dkr, 360skr, 330nkr, 150zł, USA $50, Can $60, Aus $84, NZ $99, ¥6,900, 300rmb, HK$410, RM185, SG$70

IDONETH DEEPKIN NAMARTI THRALLS

Available: Now

£30, €40, 300dkr, 360skr, 330nkr, 150zł, USA $50, Can $60, Aus $84, NZ $99, ¥6,900, 300rmb, HK$410, RM185, SG$70

ISHARANN AGENTS AND THE EIDOLON OF MATHLANN

**IDONETH DEEPKIN
ISHARANN
TIDECASTER**

Pre-order: Now
Available: 05 May

£15, €20, 150dkr,
180skr, 170nkr, 75zł,
USA $25, Can $30,
Aus $40, NZ $50,
¥3,500, 150rmb,
HK$200, RM90,
SG$35

**IDONETH DEEPKIN
ISHARANN
SOULSCRYER**

Pre-order: Now
Available: 05 May

£15, €20, 150dkr,
180skr, 170nkr, 75zł,
USA $25, Can $30,
Aus $40, NZ $50,
¥3,500, 150rmb,
HK$200, RM90,
SG$35

The mystical Isharann have important roles to play in battle, for without them souls could not be found and captured and the undersea beasts of the Akhelians would flounder on dry land.

There are four plastic characters for the Idoneth Isharann – the Tidecaster (1), Soulscryer (2), Soulrender (3) and Lotann, Warden of the Soul Ledgers (4). The Tidecaster is a powerful battle wizard and a master of arcane energy. Armed with a pelagic staff and brandishing the aelven rune of water in her outstretched hand, she advances into the heart of the enemy army, bringing the crushing weight of the ethersea down upon them. The Soulscryer is essential to the success of an Idoneth raid. With his cyfar compass and dowserchimes he traces paths through the ethersea in search of souls, the ethereal scryfish around him flickering in

and out of sight as they hunt for new prey. When suitable souls are discovered, it is the Soulrender who steps in to claim them, reaping those who have yet to die with his talúnhook and ensnaring the souls of the deceased with the lurelight that hangs from his helm. Lotann, meanwhile, records every soul successfully captured and every soul lost in battle. Protected by his Ochtar familiar, he is meticulous in his record-keeping, for the lives of many Idoneth rely on his diligence.

Over the Isharann looms the Eidolon of Mathlann (5), a collective manifestation of Idoneth spirits that have coalesced into the image of their fallen god. Here you can see the Eidolon as the Aspect of the Sea, though the kit also makes the more vengeful Aspect of the Storm. You can see more of all these kits in Designers' Notes on page 28.

AKHELIAN KINGS AND HIGH KING VOLTURNOS

When the Idoneth go to war it is the Akhelian Kings that lead them. Having earned their status through merit rather than birth, they are fearsome warriors and masterful tacticians, knowing exactly when to launch an assault and when to step in and lead from the front. As a sign of their noble standing, they ride to battle atop fearsome Deepmares, one of the few undersea creatures that willingly ally themselves to the Idoneth. This plastic kit enables you to build either an Akhelian King (1) or the special character Volturnos, High King of the Deep (2). Volturnos wields Astra Solus, the blade of light, and behind his head you can see the Crest of the High Kings, which features Volturnos' rune in its centre. The Akhelian King, meanwhile, comes with several modelling options including three unique heads and a choice of weapons – either a bladed polearm or a greatsword. The Akhelian King's mount also has a different head to the one ridden by Volturnos.

GLOOMTIDE SHIPWRECK

When the Idoneth Deepkin go to war, they are surrounded by the ethersea, a magical creation summoned by the Isharann Tidecasters. Within this sea spectral fish flit by, coral erupts from the ground and ancient shipwrecks lurk in the gloom. This plastic kit includes one such shipwreck, which you can use as scenery in your games, complete with its own rules which you can find in Battletome: Idoneth Deepkin. The set also includes six shoals of fish for use on this or any of your Idoneth models.

IDONETH DEEPKIN ISHARANN SOULRENDER

Pre-order: Now
Available: 05 May

£15, €20, 150dkr, 180skr, 170nkr, 75zł, USA $25, Can $30, Aus $40, NZ $50, ¥3,500, 150rmb, HK$200, RM90, SG$35

IDONETH DEEPKIN LOTANN, WARDEN OF THE SOUL LEDGERS

Available: Now

£20, €25, 200dkr, 240skr, 220nkr, 100zł, USA $35, Can $40, Aus $55, NZ $65, ¥4,600, 200rmb, HK$270, RM125, SG$50

IDONETH DEEPKIN EIDOLON OF MATHLANN

Available: Now

£65, €85, 650dkr, 780skr, 720nkr, 325zł, USA $110, Can $130, Aus $180, NZ $215, ¥15,000, 650rmb, HK$880, RM400, SG$155

IDONETH DEEPKIN VOLTURNOS, HIGH KING OF THE DEEP

Available: Now

£25, €32.50, 250dkr, 300skr, 280nkr, 125zł, USA $40, Can $50, Aus $70, NZ $83, ¥5,800, 250rmb, HK$340, RM155, SG$60

ETHERIC VORTEX: GLOOMTIDE SHIPWRECK

Available: Now

£25, €32.50, 250dkr, 300skr, 280nkr, 125zł, USA $40, Can $50, Aus $70, NZ $83, ¥5,800, 250rmb, HK$340, RM155, SG$60

IDONETH DEEPKIN AKHELIAN GUARD

Pre-order: 12 May
Available: 19 May

£30, €40, 300dkr, 360skr, 330nkr, 150zł, USA $50, Can $60, Aus $84, NZ $99, ¥6,900, 300rmb, HK$410, RM185, SG$70

IDONETH DEEPKIN AKHELIAN ALLOPEX

Pre-order: 12 May
Available: 19 May

£27.50, €35, 280dkr, 340skr, 300nkr, 140zł, USA $45, Can $55, Aus $77, NZ $90, ¥6,300, 280rmb, HK$370, RM170, SG$65

IDONETH DEEPKIN AKHELIAN LEVIADON

Pre-order: 05 May
Available: 12 May

£70, €90, 700dkr, 840skr, 770nkr, 350zł, USA $115, Can $140, Aus $190, NZ $230, ¥16,100, 700rmb, HK$950, RM435, SG$170

NEW PAINTS

Available: Now

£2.55, €3.30, 30dkr, 35skr, 35nkr, 13zł, USA $4.25, Can $5, Aus $6, NZ $7, ¥550, 25rmb, HK$35, RM16, SG$6

Available exclusively from games-workshop.com.

THE AKHELIAN CAVALRY

Following in the wake of the Namarti assault are the Akhelians, the warrior cadres of the Idoneth enclaves. Unlike the Namarti, every Akhelian has a strong aelven soul and they will live for many ages, enabling them to hone their martial skills in battle. Where the Namarti fight on foot, the Akhelians ride into battle on vicious mounts – sea creatures and monsters that have been bound to their will by the magic of the Isharann. Most take Fangmora Eels as their mounts, while others ride even larger and more ferocious sea creatures.

There are three plastic kits available for the Akhelians – the Akhelian Guard (1), the Akhelian Allopex (2) and the Akhelian Leviadon (see opposite). The Akhelian Guard kit contains three models, which can be built either as Ishlaen Guard armed with helsabres and galv-shields or Morrsarr Guard equipped with voltspears and galv-shields. There are different helmets for each unit – crested for the Morsarr, bladed for the Ishlaen – plus options to build a Lochian Prince to lead the unit, a standard bearer and a musician blowing a conch.

The Akhelian Allopex is a fierce predator of the sea and large enough to carry two Akhelians into battle, one as a rider, the other as a gunner for a razorshell harpoon launcher. Like the Fangmora Eels, the Allopex wears armour over its eyes to ensure it stays tame, while a rune of Mathlann has been carved into its flank to show the Idoneth's dominance over it. There are two heads for the Allopex and the harpoon launcher can be swapped for a retarius net launcher. The kit also includes loads of optional extras such as bottles, nets, a grapnel and a quiver of harpoons.

SEE ALL THE NEW IDONETH DEEPKIN MODELS IN ACTION ON PAGE 72

AKHELIAN LEVIADON

The Leviadon is one of the larger attack creatures used by the Idoneth in their raids. A monster from the darkest depths of the oceans, a Leviadon is a living battering ram that can shatter an enemy battleline in one ferocious charge. Yet the Leviadon does not fight alone, for atop its barnacle-encrusted shell sits a fighting platform crewed by no less than four Idoneth aelves. A battle-scarred Akhelian known as a Ma'harr steers the blinded beast into battle, while two Akhelian crew fire harpoon launchers from the panniers on either side of the platform. On a raised dais at the back of the Leviadon stands a Namarti Void Drummer, who beats out a tempo that sends ripples through the ethersea, distorting the outline of the Leviadon and Idoneth units nearby. This huge plastic kit comes with a variety of options including two heads for the Leviadon and flippers that can be mounted on either side of the model for more posing options. The Leviadon frame also includes loads of extra parts such as satchels, vials, soul ledgers and a cauldron.

NEW PAINTS

You can't have failed to notice that the Idoneth Namarti have suspiciously pale, almost translucent skin – we reckon this is on account of their withering souls. To help you achieve this look on your own Idoneth models, there are two new paints available this month – Ionrach Skin and Deepkin Flesh. Ionrach Skin is a new Base paint perfect for basecoating your Namarti Thralls and Reavers. You can then use the Deepkin Flesh Layer paint to highlight their muscles. Make sure you check out Paint Splatter on page 120, where we show you how to use these paints in conjunction with the existing range to paint a Namarti Thrall.

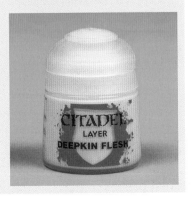

ALIENS AND ALIEN HUNTERS

The Deathwatch are the Imperium's final line of defence against the alien hordes that seek to destroy humanity. This month, the Deathwatch get a brand-new codex, but they'll have their work cut out for them because the mysterious Harlequins have a new codex, too!

CODEX: DEATHWATCH

Pre-order: 05 May
Available: 12 May

£25, €32.50, 250dkr, 300skr, 280nkr, 125zł, USA $40, Can $50, Aus $70, NZ $83, ¥5,800, 250rmb, HK$340, RM155, SG$60

Available in English, French and German languages. An abridged edition is available in Italian and Spanish. See www.games-workshop.com for more information.

CODEX: DEATHWATCH COLLECTORS' EDITION

Pre-order: 05 May
Available: 12 May

£50, €65, 500dkr, 600skr, 550nkr, 250zł, USA $80, Can $100, Aus $140, NZ $165, ¥11,500, 500rmb, HK$680, RM310, SG$120

Available exclusively from games-workshop.com.

CODEX: HARLEQUINS

Pre-order: 12 May
Available: 19 May

£20, €25, 200dkr, 240skr, 220nkr, 100zł, USA $35, Can $40, Aus $55, NZ $65, ¥4,600, 200rmb, HK$270, RM125, SG$50

Available in English, French and German languages. An abridged edition is available in Italian and Spanish. See www.games-workshop.com for more information.

CODEX: HARLEQUINS COLLECTORS' EDITION

Pre-order: 12 May
Available: 19 May

£50, €65, 500dkr, 600skr, 550nkr, 250zł, USA $80, Can $100, Aus $140, NZ $165, ¥11,500, 500rmb, HK$680, RM310, SG$120

Available exclusively from games-workshop.com.

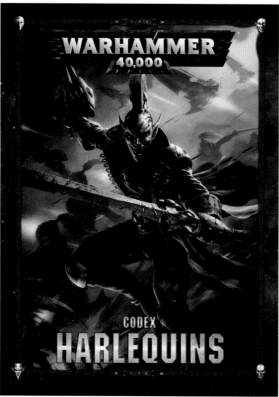

CODEX: DEATHWATCH

The Deathwatch are the Imperium's ultimate xenos-hunters. Their ranks are made up of veteran Space Marines from every Chapter – warriors who have shown an aptitude for hunting down and purging hostile alien lifeforms. Deployed in small but powerful Kill Teams, the forces of the Deathwatch are often outnumbered but never outgunned, as they wield some of the most powerful weapons and equipment available to the armies of the Imperium.

Codex: Deathwatch is a 104-page tome containing everything you need to know about these infamous alien-killers. Inside, you can read about the history of the Deathwatch, from their creation right up to the Ultimaris Decree where their ranks were bolstered by the Primaris Space Marines. The codex contains all the rules for using a Deathwatch army in your games of Warhammer 40,000, from units entries, wargear lists and points values to warlord traits, stratagems and relics. You'll also find an inspirational miniatures gallery in the book showcasing the Deathwatch range.

CODEX: HARLEQUINS

The Aeldari have many unusual factions, from Craftworlders and Exodites to Corsairs and Drukhari. Yet arguably the most unusual of the Aeldari are the Harlequins, who record and recount the history of their race through extravagant dances that they perform on the battlefield, leaping, diving, running and swooping through the enemy flanks, leaving confusion, sorrow, horror and death in their wake.

This 80-page codex tells you all about the Harlequins, from their worship of the Laughing God Cegorach to the many different masques that perform across the length and breadth of the galaxy. The codex also features a very colourful miniatures gallery filled with pictures of exquisitely painted Harlequins (so many diamonds!) and example colour schemes for all the major masques. The rest of the book is dedicated to rules, including warlord traits, relics, stratagems, tactical objectives, Forms (battle tactics) for six well-known masques and unit entries for all the models in the Harlequins range.

FIVE THINGS WE LOVE IN... MAY

3 Big battles! We're playing two Battle Reports this month, one each for Warhammer Age of Sigmar and Warhammer 40,000. In one we pit the forces of Death against the Idoneth Deepkin in a battle for lost souls. In the other, Space Marines and T'au take to the field in a four-player game.

2 Classic games. This month heralds the release of not only a new Necromunda Gang – the Van Saar – but also a new Blood Bowl team in the shape of the Doom Lords. Both come with accessories – gang cards and dice for the Van Saar and a new Chaos-tainted pitch for the Doom Lords. Gang War 3 is also out this month for Necromunda – wowsers!

DATACARDS: DEATHWATCH

You know the drill with datacards by now, right? If you're playing games with the Deathwatch you'll definitely want to pick up this set of 74 cards, which contains 36 tactical objectives for use in Maelstrom of War missions, seven psychic power cards (six from the Librarius discipline and Smite) and 31 stratagems including several that can be used against specific alien threats. Can you guess what Stem the Green Tide could be used against?

DATACARDS: HARLEQUINS

If you're picking up a copy of Codex: Harlequins then you'll want to get a set of datacards for them, too. This set of 71 cards contains 36 tactical objectives and seven psychic powers (six from the Phantasmancy discipline plus Smite). It also includes cards for the three stratagems in the core rules, plus 25 unique ones for the Harlequins. The War Dancers stratagem is especially nasty, though we also really like the Shrieking Doom card.

DATACARDS: DEATHWATCH

Pre-order: 05 May
Available: 12 May

£10, €12, 100dkr, 120skr, 110nkr, 50zł, USA $15, Can $20, Aus $28, NZ $33, ¥2,300, 100rmb, HK$140, RM60, SG$24

Available in English, French, German, Italian and Spanish languages.

DATACARDS: HARLEQUINS

Pre-order: 12 May
Available: 19 May

£10, €12, 100dkr, 120skr, 110nkr, 50zł, USA $15, Can $20, Aus $28, NZ $33, ¥2,300, 100rmb, HK$140, RM60, SG$24

Available in English, French, German, Italian and Spanish languages.

AELDARI WEBWAY GATE

Pre-order: 19 May
Available: 26 May

£25, €32.50, 250dkr, 300skr, 280nkr, 125zł, USA $40, Can $50, Aus $70, NZ $83, ¥5,800, 250rmb, HK$340, RM155, SG$60

AELDARI WEBWAY GATE

Webway Gates are ancient wraithbone constructs that enable access to spars of the Aeldari Webway. Normally hidden by alien magicks, Webway Gates shimmer into existence when activated, Aeldari units surging through the glowing portal to engage the enemy. This plastic kit is the perfect addition to any Aeldari army or Warhammer 40,000 scenery collection. It has a classic, curved Aeldari aesthetic based on artwork from Codex: Craftworlds with wraith constructs standing sentinel on the outsides of the gate's arms. At 13" tall, the Webway Gate is easily large enough to fit a Wraithknight beneath it. The rules for the Webway Gate come in the kit, though they can also be found in Codex: Harlequins.

BLOOD BOWL MERCHANDISE

"Wow! Can you hear the cheering, Bob? The Doom Lords are making their way onto the pitch for the first time this season and it's a rapturous reception. What does rapturous mean? It means the crowd are excited, Bob, really excited. And you can see why!"

SPIKE! JOURNAL

The Spike! Journal is a 36-page illustrated sports magazine – an in-world artefact that every Blood Bowl fan would carry in their back pocket to their next match. This edition is all about the Chaos Chosen and features background on the teams and stats for all the players (essentially, the rules for Chaos Chosen teams). Inside you'll also find stats and interviews with famous Star Players such as Lord Borak, a Doom Lords painting guide, a playbook packed with useful tactics, new rules for using Wizards in Blood Bowl and even a brand-new comic strip by classic Blood Bowl artist Pete Knifton.

MANY DICE, MORE CARDS

There's not one set of Blood Bowl dice out this month, but three – one each for the Underworld Denizens, Chaos Renegades and Chaos Chosen teams (an example of which you can see below). Each set contains seven Blood Bowl dice in their team colours. Also out this month are team Card packs for the Chaos Chosen and the Skaven, each of which contains 44 game cards.

THE DOOM LORDS

The Doom Lords are one of the most infamous Chaos Chosen teams in the known world, having butchered, slaughtered, maimed, killed and, occasionally, scored their way to victory in countless Blood Bowl matches over the years. As the 2486 NAF AFC North divisional Champions, the 2493 Chaos Cup Champions and the sole survivors of the Halfing Thimble League, they have certainly made a name for themselves.

This plastic set includes 12 Chaos Chosen team members (four Chosen Blockers and eight Beastmen), six balls, two score coins and two turn markers. The Chosen Blockers are, as you'd expect, suitably beefy individuals, with bulging muscles and plenty of armour (not for their own protection, we'll have you know, but for smashing apart rival players). The heads are interchangeable between the four models. The eight Beastmen, meanwhile, are a little more lithe but no less dangerous, for they can skewer their opponents with their horns when they Blitz. Always handy when you need someone to clear a path for the ball. The Beastmen all have interchangeable heads and horns, giving you plenty of variety between your players.

The set also comes with a one million gold piece team roster for the Doom Lords for those of you that want to play straight out of the box.

OPTIONAL RULE: CHAOS CHOSEN SPECIAL BALLS

These rules allow Chaos Chosen teams to make use of their own special balls, and is designed to be used alongside the rules for other teams' special balls (previously published in White Dwarf and now to be found in the Inaugural Blood Bowl Almanac, too). As with all optional rules, the use of these balls set should be agreed between both coaches in one-off games, and their use in league play is at the League Commissioner's discretion.

Once per match, at the start of any drive for which they are the kicking team, the Chaos Chosen coach can declare that they will use the either the Daemonic Ball or the Orb of Dark Majesty. If they wish, they can use an Extra Spiky Ball (see the March 2017 issue of White Dwarf or the Inaugural Blood Bowl Almanac) instead – they should declare which ball they are using before any players are set up.

Before the kick-off, the coach nominates one player from their team who is on the pitch, is not in a wide zone and is not on the line of scrimmage to be the one kicking the ball. (Note that in some situations, such as using the Kick skill, a player will already have been nominated to kick the ball). If the roll on the Kick-off table is a double, the Ref calls the kicking player out for their flagrant rules violation, and they are immediately sent off as though they had committed a foul (before resolving the kick-off result). Note that even if the player is sent off, the special ball remains in play for this drive!

For the duration of the drive, the special rules for the ball in use (as shown below) apply to the ball. Aside from those, it still counts as a normal ball in all respects.

If a second ball ever comes into play, it will be a regulation Blood Bowl ball. Things are mad enough without multiple special balls on the pitch!

DAEMONIC BALL

In ages past mighty champions of Chaos would bind foul daemons into weapons of war, making hideous tools of destruction that would consume the souls of the fallen. These days the weapons may have changed but the horror of encountering a bound daemon has not!

Before making any attempt to Pick-up this ball, roll a D6. On a roll of 1 the player quails in fear from the Daemonic thing and refuses to touch it. This does not cause a Turnover, but the ball will scatter as normal. Additionally, when a player carrying the Daemonic Ball ends their movement, and if no pass action has yet been made this turn, roll a D6. On a roll of 1 the player must attempt to pass the ball to another player on their team if possible or to an empty square if no friendly players are in passing range.

Finally, whenever this ball comes to rest after scattering, roll a D6. On a roll of a 6 the ball splits, weakening the dark enchantment and allowing the bound daemon to break free. For the remainder of the drive treat the ball as a normal, regulation Blood Bowl ball.

ORB OF DARK MAJESTY

Chaos Chosen teams will often make use of artefacts of power and icons of the Chaos Gods as balls. Infused with baleful energies, such balls are hideous to behold and all but the strongest of will can find themselves transfixed by a dark influence, losing their free will and succumbing to that of the Chaos Chosen's patrons. Any player carrying an Orb of Dark Majesty gains the Really Stupid skill. If they already are Really Stupid, they are unaffected by the influence of the Dark gods.

CHAOS CHOSEN PITCH

The Doom Lords are always eager to play an away game, but they do love a match on their home turf. Well, we say turf – it's a blasted landscape covered in sigils to the Dark Gods. And, if blood is spilt (which is virtually guaranteed), the board can be flipped over at half time to reveal chaos energy tearing through the pitch.

THE GANG WAR CONTINUES

House Van Saar are the most tech-savvy of all the houses in the Necromunda underhive, with access to devastating rad-weapons and powerful energy shields. This new gang are available now. You can find their full gang rules in Gang War 3, also out now!

VAN SAAR GANG

The gang members of House Van Saar are amongst the best-equipped fighters in the Necromunda underhive, carrying weapons and wargear that other house gangs could only dream of owning. Yet their high-tech equipment comes with a heavy price tag, because the machine that manufactures the Van Saars' arms and armour is highly unstable, slowly irradiating those who work too closely with it. For the gangers of House Van Saar it is a risk they are willing to take – house supremacy in the underhive is more important than the life of an individual. The radiation suits they wear protect them from the worst of the radiation, though most gangers require regular medical treatment to stay fit and healthy.

This plastic set contains 10 Van Saar models, enabling you to build your very own gang of high-tech underhive warriors. There are two identical sprues in the kit, each containing five ganger bodies (four male and one female) and ten heads – five bare and five helmeted. The kit also contains loads of weapons, including parts for 10 lasguns, four las carbines, two suppression lasers, two plasma guns, four laspistols, four plasma pistols, two melta-las combi-weapons (all of these gun bodies can be mated with any model's gun stock, giving you loads of construction options) two rad guns (the shoulder-mounted cannon), and two Hystrar energy shields with translucent plastic force fields.

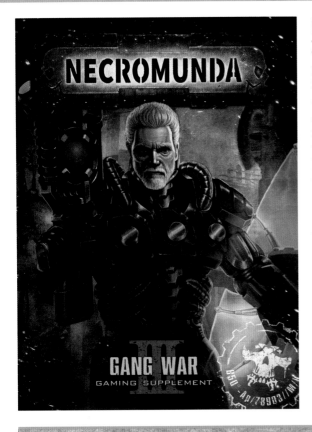

GANG WAR 3

Gang War is back for its third instalment and it is packed full of new rules for Necromunda. In fact, it's so rules heavy it's a whopping 90 pages long – a veritable feast of new gaming material. First up are the rules for House Van Saar, enabling you to field a gang using the new models presented to the left. There are new weapon and equipment lists for them, too, which include the Hystrar pattern energy shield, rad gun and suppression laser to mention but a few. Gang War 3 also includes rules for Brutes such as the Excavation Automata and the Servitor-Ogryn, three new hired guns and exotic pets such as Sumpkrocs (guess which gang makes use of them) and Phyrr Cats (ditto). The Trading Post has also been expanded significantly with weapons such as mining lasers and seismic cannons and wargear like conversion fields and hazard suits. There are also additional rules for campaigns and twelve new scenarios (two of which are multiplayer games). And that's all still just the tip of the iceberg. If you're a fan of Necromunda then you will definitely want this book for your next campaign.

GANG WAR 3

Pre-order: Now
Available: 05 May

£17.50, €22.50, 180dkr, 220skr, 190nkr, 88zl, USA $30, Can $35, Aus $49, NZ $58, ¥4,000, 180rmb, HK$240, RM110, SG$40

Available in English, French, German, Spanish, Italian, Chinese and Japanese languages.

CHECK OUT THE EXCLUSIVE RULES FOR VENATOR GANGS ON PAGE 108

WHAT'S NEW IN GANG WAR 3?

There are so many new and exciting features in Gang War 3 that we decided to catch up with Andy Hoare, the shady uphive type in charge of all things Necromunda...

White Dwarf: So, Andy, what's Gang War 3 all about?

Andy Hoare: Right from the start we wanted to make Necromunda bigger and better than it's ever been. But we didn't want it to be a facsimile of the original game by making the same gangs with the same options followed by the same game supplements. We wanted to cover some new ground early on and that's exactly what you'll find in Gang War 3.

WD: New ground? Like what?

AH: For a start, this book contains the biggest and best Trading Post ever seen on Necromunda – it is colossal, with all manner of equipment available to your gangs. You can buy seismic cannons and servo-skulls, web pistols, dum-dum rounds, combi weapons, grav guns, all the classic heavy weapons, rock saws and rock drills, gunshrouds, telescopic sights, suspensors, 10 types of grenades... the list goes on. You can paint your favourite gun gold – there's an upgrade for that!

WD: That does sound pretty comprehensive. Are all these weapons that you can get for your models, then?

AH: A lot of them will be available as upgrade packs for the different gangs, yes. We wanted there to be several levels to building your Necromunda gang – you can build a plastic gang straight out of the box. You can use the resin upgrade packs that we're bringing out to make new gang members with different equipment. Or you can use weapons and wargear from existing kits to convert your models. You can find rock drills and saws in the Genestealer Cults Acolyte Hybrids set, for example and web guns and heavy stubbers in the Neophytes kit.

WD: What other new ground have you covered then?

AH: We've introduced Brutes. These are kind of like the big guys in Blood Bowl. In this book you'll find the 'Ambot' Excavation Automata and the Servitor-Ogryn – industrial slave machines that have been stolen, rebuilt and repurposed by the gangs. You'll also find pets for each of the four gangs out so far – the Caryatid, for example, has been a part of Necromunda's background since it was called Confrontation! Trish has made a great little model of it, too. Probably the biggest thing, though, is the introduction of an arbitrated campaign. By that we mean that you have a neutral gamesmaster to run your campaign who ensures the storyline plays out smoothly. There are 12 new scenarios in the book for the gamesmaster to use (though they can be used for regular battles without a gamesmaster). We feel they add an extra level to the depth of the game, giving you more flavour, more narrative and more crunch. You really get to explore the depths of the setting more and create a story between you and your gaming buddies.

LICENSED GAMES

All across the world, our licensed partners are creating fantastic new games based on Games Workshop's tabletop games. This month, big news for fans of Warhammer Fantasy Roleplay, and first sighting of Adeptus Titanicus and Aeronautica Imperialis!

A HISTORY OF WARHAMMER ROLEPLAY

Warhammer Fantasy Roleplay was first published by Games Workshop in 1986. It played a pivotal role in establishing much of the history and detail of the Old World, away from the battlefield. There's been two editions since, but for many the original first edition and the second edition which followed in 2005 represent the classic editions of the game, and it's these that Cubicle 7's new edition draws from.

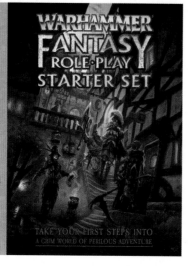

WARHAMMER FANTASY ROLEPLAY

If you haven't heard, a new edition of Warhammer Fantasy Roleplay is on the way from Cubicle 7 Entertainment and should be with us any time now. This new edition will return players to Warhammer's grim world of perilous adventure, with updated, fourth edition rules (more on those to the left). For those new to the game (or, indeed, the world of roleplaying), players take on the guise of an individual character of their choosing, working with their fellow players to overcome the many challenges set by the gamesmaster as they adventure in the Old World.

Not only will Cubicle 7 be releasing a new edition of the game but they'll also be returning some of the game's most famed adventures to print. But, if it's possible, there's even bigger news than that – the folks at Cubicle 7 are also working on a brand-new companion game to Warhammer Fantasy Roleplay – the Age of Sigmar Roleplaying Game, also expected this year! We spoke to Cubicle 7 Design Lead Dominic McDowall about these two projects.

Graeme Davis (who worked on the original Warhammer Fantasy Roleplay all the way back in the 1980s) is working on the project. What has Graeme been able to contribute?
It's been awesome working with Graeme, he brings a fantastic depth of knowledge and expertise to the project. I'm a huge fan of the original game, so Graeme was always going to be a part of the development dream team. He's got some great stories to tell in the Old World, and I can't wait to share them with you. It's a huge honour to be working with him on the Director's Cut of the classic Enemy Within campaign.

You're working on both Old World and Age of Sigmar incarnations of the game at the same time. How is that working out and have the projects influenced each other?
It's been fascinating to work on two such contrasting fantasy settings with threads of continuity between them. Something I think we do really well is make roleplaying games that capture the feel of their setting, so we are focusing on the different strengths and flavours of each game. I've been playing games in the Old World for 30 years so it's a wonderful setting that I am extremely fond of, and Age of Sigmar is so fresh, exciting and full of potential – I think we've got the best of both worlds!

The original Warhammer Fantasy Roleplay is particularly well regarded for adding previously unimagined detail to the Warhammer World and the Old World in particular. Is that an aim with the forthcoming Age of Sigmar edition?
In the Age of Sigmar Roleplaying Game you experience the world as an individual, so we explore the Mortal Realms from a different perspective. It's hugely exciting to be able to delve into all those details – all those settlements, characters and stories out there waiting to be discovered. It's a privilege to be involved, and I can't wait to hear about everyone's adventures!

For all the latest on Warhammer Fantasy Roleplay and the forthcoming Age of Sigmar Roleplaying Game, head over to Cubicle 7's website at:

www.cubicle7.co.uk

ADEPTUS TITANICUS: DOMINUS

Available now on Steam Early Access is the excellent Adeptus Titanicus: Dominus from Membrane Studios. The game puts you in control of the greatest weapons available to the Imperium of Man, the mighty Titans of the Adeptus Titanicus, and offers an easy-to-play yet deep, strategic and tactical turn-based experience, as the gargantuan Titans exchange volleys from Volcano Cannons, Laser Blasters, Plasma Annihilators and other epic, super-powered weapons of the far-off future.

This Early Access version features a Skirmish mode against an AI opponent for single-player and an online multiplayer mode. The full release will also offer an exciting single-player campaign. For more information, visit adeptustitanicus-dominus.com.

LATEST FROM FORGE WORLD

Forge World make highly detailed resin models, large-scale kits and books that explore the worlds of Warhammer 40,000 and Warhammer Age of Sigmar. Their offering this month is the Termite, a deadly drilling war machine from the time of the Great Crusade.

THE TERMITE

The Terrax Pattern Termite Assault Drill is a specialised transport vehicle designed to deliver a squad of troops into the heart of an enemy fortress while bypassing walls, turret guns and defenders. Upon delivering its cargo, the Termite will be used to target enemy bunkers and bastions, reducing them to rubble with its spinning drill-head and melta-cutter array. The Termite can be used by Legiones Astartes, Imperialis Militia and Mechanicum units in games of Warhammer 40,000: Age of Darkness.

FORGE WORLD

This kit and the rest of the Forge World range of miniatures are available directly from Forge World. To find out more visit:

forgeworld.co.uk

A CAREER
LIKE NO OTHER

GAMES WORKSHOP IS HIRING RETAIL STORE MANAGERS.

DO YOU WANT TO RUN YOUR OWN GAMES WORKSHOP STORE?

ARE YOU EXCITED ABOUT DELIVERING AN AMAZING CUSTOMER EXPERIENCE TO EVERY PERSON WHO WALKS THROUGH YOUR DOOR?

Visit jobs.games-workshop.com to find the latest opportunities in your area, and all current vacanacies in every part of Games Workshop.

Be part of the hobby you love.

TALES FROM THE BLACK LIBRARY

Black Library produce novels, audiobooks, compilations and short stories set in the universes of Warhammer Age of Sigmar and Warhammer 40,000. This month, Dwarfs and Elves battle in the Old World, the Horus Heresy rages on and Neferata spills some blood.

WOLFSBANE
Pre-order: 12 May
Available: 19 May

£20, €25, 200dkr, 240skr, 240nkr, 100zł, USA $30, Can $35, Aus $45, NZ $50, ¥2,600, 220rmb, HK$272, RM124, SG$48

SALAMANDERS: THE OMNIBUS
Pre-order: 05 May
Available: 12 May

£15, €20, 145dkr, 175skr, 175nkr, 74.95zł, USA $21, Can $25, Aus $30, NZ $35, ¥1,750, 120rmb, HK$205, RM95, SG$35

THE WAR OF VENGEANCE OMNIBUS
Pre-order: 19 May
Available: 26 May

£15, €20, 145dkr, 175skr, 175nkr, 74.95zł, USA $21, Can $25, Aus $30, NZ $35, ¥1,750, 120rmb, HK$205, RM95, SG$35

NEFERATA, MORTARCH OF BLOOD SPECIAL EDITION
Pre-order: 12 May
Available: 19 May

£40, €55, 400dkr, 480skr, 440nkr, 200zł, USA $65, Can $80, Aus $90, NZ $130, ¥9,200, 400rmb, HK$540, RM250, SG$95

Available exclusively from blacklibrary.com.

THE VOICE OF MARS
Pre-order: Now
Available: 05 May

£18, €22, 180dkr, 215skr, 215nkr, 90zł, USA $27, Can $32, Aus $40, NZ $45, ¥2,340, 195rmb, HK$245, RM112, SG$43

BLACKSHIELDS: RED FIEF
Pre-order: 12 May
Available: 19 May

£12, €15, 130dkr, 160skr, 160nkr, 60zł, USA $17.50, Can $19, Aus $25, NZ $30, ¥1,400, HK$160, RM75, SG$30

FEATURED BOOK
WOLFSBANE

By Guy Haley | Hardback | 368 pages | 19 May

There's a new novel for the Horus Heresy coming out and it features the Space Wolves. For Russ and the Allfather!

Guy Haley once again applies his quill to the saga of the Horus Heresy, but this time the story is all about Leman Russ and his feral legion. With Horus now paving a way towards Holy Terra intent on conquering the galaxy, Leman Russ must make a difficult choice – to defend the home world of the Imperium alongside his brother Primarchs or strike out for Horus's forces and behead the snake before it can strike. Russ is regarded as one of the greatest warriors among the Primarchs, yet reports from Malcador's spies have suggested that Horus has become powerful beyond reckoning, infused with diabolical power. Of course, this is of no concern to Leman Russ – he has vowed to slay the Warmaster and he will not go back on his oath. But what must he sacrifice in return?

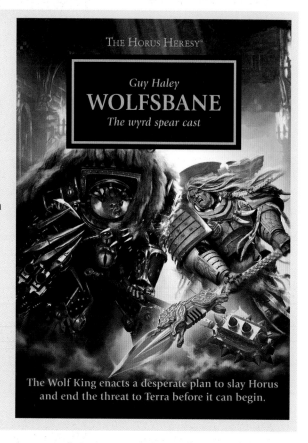

THE HORUS HERESY

Guy Haley
WOLFSBANE
The wyrd spear cast

The Wolf King enacts a desperate plan to slay Horus and end the threat to Terra before it can begin.

NEW TO OMNIBUS CORNER

There are two new Black Library omnibuses out this month – *Salamanders* by Nick Kyme and *The War of Vengeance* also by Nick Kyme (well, with the help of Chris Wraight and C.L. Werner). *Salamanders* contains the three novels from the original series (*Salamander*, *Firedrake* and *Nocturne*), plus ten short stories based around the main characters. *War of Vengeance*, meanwhile, is set in the far-distant past of the world-that-was, when the Dwarfs and Elves fought for domination of the Old World. This weighty tome includes the novels *The Great Betrayal*, *Master of Dragons* and *Curse of the Phoenix Crown*.

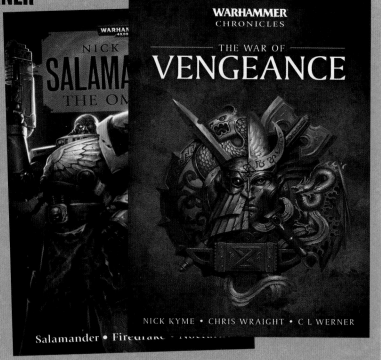

WARHAMMER CHRONICLES

THE WAR OF VENGEANCE

NICK KYME • CHRIS WRAIGHT • C L WERNER

Salamander • Firedrake

NEFERATA, MORTARCH OF BLOOD

By David Annandale | Hardback | 240 pages | 19 May

With Nagash and the forces of Death very much in the ascendancy at the moment, what better way to celebrate than with a special edition novel about one of his most infamous lieutenants – Neferata? As Shyish comes under attack from countless foes desperate to stop whatever the Great Necromancer is planning, the ancient mistress of Nulahmia must defend her city in a war that could last centuries. Prepare yourself for a tale of epic battles and undying legions in the Realm of Death.

THE VOICE OF MARS

By David Guymer | Hardback | 386 pages | 05 May

David Guymer is back with a new Iron Hands novel – The Voice of Mars! Fans of the Iron Hands may recall the Clan Raukaan codex supplement, which told of the Slaughter on Dawnbreak and the recovery by Clan Raukaan of an ancient alien artefact. This novel tells what happens next. As Iron Father Kristos investigates the relic, his warriors must pit themselves against a greenskin invasion and, then, their own brothers! On the Iron Council, the Tech-Priests known as the Voice of Mars watch on with interest…

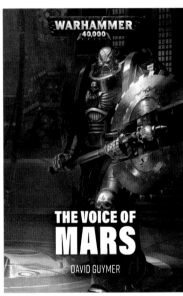

BLACKSHIELDS: RED FIEF

By Josh Reynolds | Audio Drama | 76 minutes | 19 May

The renegade World Eater Endryd Haar is back in this sequel to the popular audio drama Blackshields: The False War. Fighting neither for the Emperor or the Warmaster, Haar must find new warriors to bolster the strength of his warband or face oblivion as the Horus Heresy rages around him. If you like your Space Marines dangerous, uncompromising, with dubious morals and a worrying lack of honour (except towards fellow renegades, of course) then Blackshields: Red Fief is the perfect audio drama for you.

Many Black Library books and audio CDs – including the entire Horus Heresy series – are also available as eBooks and MP3 downloads. For more information, and to see the full range of Black Library products available, visit:

www.blacklibrary.com

THE READER'S GUIDE

GUY HALEY

Duardin, aelves, grots, Orks, Chaos warlords, Space Marines, Primarchs, tanks… Guy Haley has written about them all and more besides! His latest novel Wolfsbane is out this month – here are five more of his novels that you also might like to read.

DARK IMPERIUM
Available as a hardback and an ebook

Abaddon's 13th Black Crusade engulfed Cadia, the galaxy was torn in half by the Great Rift, the Primarch Roboute Guilliman was brought back to life by the Aeldari and the Adeptus Mechanicus. The galaxy was in turmoil. Now, Guilliman must lead the armies of Humanity – spearheaded by the Primaris Space Marines – to rescue the Imperium and, crucially, his home world of Macragge. If you're new to Warhammer 40,000, this book is a great introduction for you.

PERTURABO: THE HAMMER OF OLYMPIA
Available as a hardback, ebook and MP3 download

The Primarchs is an ongoing series of novels that focuses on the Emperor's sons. Each novel explores an aspect or story of a particular Primarch – in this case, Perturabo – giving you an insight into who they are and why they act, think and fight the way they do. Guy's portrayal of Perturabo is exceptional, taking you right back to the Primarch's troubled childhood. You begin to understand that the lure of Chaos is strong even before the events of the Horus Heresy.

THE BEHEADING
Available as a hardback, ebook and MP3 download

The Beheading is the twelfth and final novel in the Beast Arises series – an almighty conclusion to a phenomenal story that pits the armies of the Imperium against the largest Ork Waaagh! the galaxy has ever seen. In the wake of the Horus Heresy, the last thing Humanity wants is another war. But that's just what it gets! We would suggest reading the other books in the series first (Guy also wrote the fifth novel, Throneworld) so you can enjoy the full story.

CALL OF ARCHAON
Available as a paperback, ebook and MP3 download

Want to know what it takes to become one of the Everchosen's greatest warriors? Then you need to read Call of Archaon, which pits three warriors of Chaos against each other as they battle for Archaon's favour. Whether you're a long-standing hobbyist or new to the worlds of Warhammer, this book – originally a series of eight short stories compiled into one novel – is a great way to find out more about the dread armies of Chaos in Warhammer Age of Sigmar.

BANEBLADE
Available as an ebook and MP3 download

It's a novel about a super-heavy Astra Militarum tank that's covered in guns, stuck in a sandstorm and fighting a horde of Orks! What more could you want? The best bit is, the story's not all told from the point of view of the humans safe inside their big tank – it's also told from the point of view of the Orks trying to destroy it. If you love either of these factions, you'll want to read this book. Don't forget to check out the sequel, Shadowsword!

CONTACT

Where you get to have your say... send us your letters and pictures and we'll print the best ones we get!

By submitting letters, articles or photographs, you give Games Workshop permission to feature them in White Dwarf at any time in the future.

TEAM@WHITEDWARF.CO.UK

THE WHITE DWARF BUNKER
GAMES WORKSHOP
LENTON
NOTTINGHAM
NG7 2WS
UNITED KINGDOM

THE CHANGER OF WAYS

I am halfway through collecting a Tzeentch army, comprised of mortals, Arcanites and Daemons. I hope to convert a few Magisters from the 'Battle Wizards' set, and wanted to know what the Free Cities and Stormcasts' view were on faithful scribes converting to a more chaotic deity such as Tzeentch.

Also, I love the new Necromunda models, and I hope to get a Goliath set to convert into Chaos Chosen. I can't help but ask if there was ever a Warhammer Fantasy or Age of Sigmar version of Necromunda. I did some research and found Mordheim. Will it be re-released? If so, could you please put some Tzeentch in the boxed set?

Jessie Fletcher,
Liverpool, UK

So, to answer your first question, Jessie – we imagine they would be furious!

As for Mordheim, it may return one day, but we certainly can't guarantee that. In the meantime, have you tried playing Warhammer Age of Sigmar: Skirmish? It's a great way to start a small Tzeentch warband.

WRITE TO US!

Readers! White Dwarf wants your letters, so get in touch by writing to us at: team@whitedwarf.co.uk!

Or visit us on our Facebook page (head over to Facebook and search for 'White Dwarf magazine').

STAR LETTER

MORE MISSIONS, MORE QUESTS!

Hello there and greetings from France! I've been a huge fan of the hobby since the 1990s when, as a kid, I played HeroQuest. I've got every French issue of White Dwarf since #4, and I've followed the magazine through every rise and fall. I'm glad because the White Dwarf of today is just like the old-school golden-age ones I remember from when I was younger! It has Battle Reports, hobby tips, background – you're doing a great job! The only thing you need to do to make White Dwarf even better is to include more support for Games Workshop's boxed games – some new adventures for Warhammer Quest, with new tiles and villains (remember the Skaven sewers in August 1996?). The group could fight in a necropolis filled with flesh-eating ghouls, perhaps. And please don't forget Betrayal at Calth and Burning of Prospero – you could have the Gal Vorbak fighting Invictarii Suzerains? And would the Khenetai defeat the Grey Slayers? You could even do a Space Hulk-style mission with space marines and Adeptus Custodes fighting the Sons of Horus aboard the *Vengeful Spirit* – that would be really cool!

Jeremy Owen,
Villefranche, France

Hey, Jeremy, thanks for getting in touch. We're glad you're enjoying the magazine – we really are trying to make it a magazine for all hobbyists, be they new initiates or long-standing veterans like yourself.

With regards to new missions for our boxed games, that is something we're definitely working on. You may well have seen the three Warhammer Quest missions we published in December, January and February, and the Space Hulk mission that was also in December's issue. We haven't done so much for Betrayal at Calth and Burning of Prospero for a little while. Perhaps we should! We will look into it for you. And there'll certainly be more new rules soon.

PAINTING QUESTION: SORROWFUL DIAMONDS

Dear Best Publishing Team in the World. What paints should I use for the hood and diamonds on the Harlequin Skyweavers from the Masque of the Midnight Sorrow? My wife reckons the highlight on the hood is Screamer Pink. I'm not so sure. Any advice?

Michał Chyczewski, Warsaw, Poland

Oh dear, Michał, you should have listened to your wife – it is Screamer Pink! The jetbike was undercoated Chaos Black, then the edges of the hood (and other lilac-coloured areas) were carefully highlighted with Screamer Pink and Slaanesh Grey. The diamond pattern was then painted across the top of the hood using the colours shown below. Hope that helps!

BLACK HOOD	RED DIAMONDS
Screamer Pink — Highlight	Khorne Red — Basecoat
Slaanesh Grey — Edge Highlight	Mephiston Red — Layer
	Evil Sunz Scarlet — Layer
	Fire Dragon Bright — Layer

A useful tip when applying thin edge highlights to an armour panel is to use the edge of the brush rather than the tip – it gives you better control. For the diamond pattern, try drawing it onto the jetbike with a pencil first to get the pattern right.

PROUD DAD!

You must get this all the time, but I am so proud of my son Connor's latest model. He is nearly 13 and he has been painting for three months now – he has progressed rapidly from his first attempt. Here's a picture of his Lord of Contagion to show off his newly found skills.

Gareth Dickin,
Holbeach, UK

That is seriously impressive work right there, Gareth – a hearty well done to Connor for his achievement, he certainly paints better than most of us did at his age! We're slightly suspicious of what might be in the background of the picture, though – it looks a bit like intestines… Tell Connor to keep up the great work and to remember the advice we gave him at the Warhammer 40,000 Open Day last year. We expect to see him again at a Golden Demon event in the near future!

A STRESSLESS PAINTJOB

After many years away from the hobby (I last played when I was 15, I think), I recently decided to come back, mostly due to the fact that painting models relaxes me and, in my line of work, stress can lead to very costly mistakes (*we dare not ask!* – E*d*)! So every now and then I walk into my local Games Workshop store and buy a random model that I like the look of, or a boxed game that I like all the miniatures in (good job on Blightwar, by the way, that Nurgle Daemon on the snail is brilliant), and do some painting.

Anyway, since I enjoy painting, I also started reading White Dwarf again to get some inspiration with regards to possible colour schemes, painting effects and base designs. While reading one of the issues I noticed your Readers' Models section and decided to email you a picture of one of the

models I painted recently – a Bastiladon that my wife got me for my birthday. Perhaps it will be worthy of showing in White Dwarf?

Marcin Stangel,
Maidenhead, UK

Glad to have you back in the fold, Marcin. It's always nice to get some relaxation time and a lot of us here agree with you that painting is a great way to do just that. Just don't mix up your painting water and your cup of tea – that's not so much fun. We also think your bastiladon looks brilliant – keep up the great work!

MORE RULES!

I remember White Dwarf as being a great source for new rules and you guys have done a great job introducing additional rules for boxed games like Imperial Knights: Renegade and Gangs of Commorragh. I think it would also be great if we could get some new rules for units like Colonel Schaeffer's Last Chancers or Gaunt's Ghosts for the new edition of Warhammer 40,000. How about it?

Tom Lawlor,
West Wales

Hey, Tom. We aim to include new rules for our games whenever we can, but as far as we know there are no plans for the Last Chancers or the Ghosts. Maybe one day they'll get their own rules, but sadly none of us can see into the future (or the Studio) to find out.

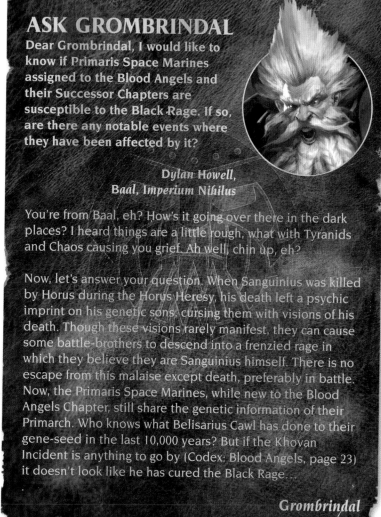

ASK GROMBRINDAL

Dear Grombrindal, I would like to know if Primaris Space Marines assigned to the Blood Angels and their Successor Chapters are susceptible to the Black Rage. If so, are there any notable events where they have been affected by it?

Dylan Howell,
Baal, Imperium Nihilus

You're from Baal, eh? How's it going over there in the dark places? I heard things are a little rough, what with Tyranids and Chaos causing you grief. Ah well, chin up, eh?

Now, let's answer your question. When Sanguinius was killed by Horus during the Horus Heresy, his death left a psychic imprint on his genetic sons, cursing them with visions of his death. Though these visions rarely manifest, they can cause some battle-brothers to descend into a frenzied rage in which they believe they are Sanguinius himself. There is no escape from this malaise except death, preferably in battle. Now, the Primaris Space Marines, while new to the Blood Angels Chapter, still share the genetic information of their Primarch. Who knows what Belisarius Cawl has done to their gene-seed in the last 10,000 years? But if the Khovan Incident is anything to go by (Codex: Blood Angels, page 23) it doesn't look like he has cured the Black Rage…

Grombrindal

TEMPORAL DISTORT

Join us on a journey through time and space, into the past of White Dwarf. This month, we find ourselves back in October 2006...

White Dwarf has a habit of going green every once in a while. No one really knows how or why it happens, but it seems to happen pretty much every time the greenskins – be they Orcs, Orks, Orruks or mere Grots – show up. (*Look at these two pages – it's just happened again! Who keeps doing this?! – Ed*) 'Orctober' 2006's White Dwarf 322 was one such occasion when a new edition of Warhammer Armies: Orcs & Goblins and a new range of greenskins for Warhammer ushered in another (mercifully temporary) takeover, with a veritable horde of Orcy features, as you can see below.

It wasn't quite all greenskins, though, with a massive *Lord of the Rings* Strategy Battle Game campaign, a Warhammer 40,000 tactica and a preview of the forthcoming Codex: Eldar, too.

BE A WINNER GO GREEN!

THE GREEN MENACE
The staff of Games Workshop Romford clearly knew which side to throw their lot in with, having built and painted this 'uge greenskin horde in preparation for the arrival of the new army book.

TIME FOR A RUMBLE?
When it is not time for a rumble, if you're an Orc? "The one major defining feature of greenskins is their seemingly endless capacity for fighting," as we noted at the time. And yet, as games designer Mat Ward explained in this feature, somehow the games development time found a way to make them even more hitty...

BASH UP IN DA SOUTHLANDS
...and how do you prove it? In da Battle Report, of course! Mark Latham (later a White Dwarf editor himself) took control of the greenskins against Andy Hoare and the Lizardmen in a 4,000-point rumble. The result? Total carnage by turn one and "A solid victory to the Orcs and Goblins!" by the end. "Orcs is da best!"

TACTICA: WALKERS

You put one foot in front of the other, then you… Oh, *walkers*, not walking. It's a bit more complicated than that, then. Fortunately, White Dwarf was here with six pages of top tips on getting the most out of everything from Space Marine Dreadnoughts to Tyranid Carnifexes and Chaos Defilers.

RAVENING HORDES

Earlier in 2006, the world had seen the coming of the seventh edition of Warhammer. With the release still fresh in the memory, White Dwarf took a look at all 14 of the races players could choose from back then. "Choose the host in whose future victories you will surely revel!" we said. You'd never see a mouthful of a sentence like that in White Dwarf these days, right?

JERVIS IS PHIL'S STANDARD BEARER

Jervis's famed monthly column spread the love this month, with a preview of the then-upcoming Codex: Eldar by Phil Kelly, complete with some hefty praise from Jervis. We hear he's still waiting for Phil to repay the favour. (*Just kidding*. – Ed)

THE RECLAMATION OF MORIA

This issue featured a huge *Middle-earth* campaign made up of six scenarios. Even more impressively, each was shown with its own custom-built board – a hefty challenge for most of us, it has to be said, but really inspirational stuff.

'EAVY METAL AND LIVIN' METAL

The issue featured not one but two 'Eavy Metal articles – one on "the mysterious, ever-living Necrontyr" and a second on characters and warriors from *The Two Towers*, including Aragorn, Legolas, the Ents of Fangorn and an Orthanc diorama featuring Saruman and Grima Wormtongue.

THIS MONTH IN…

What's this? A Legio Custodes army from *2006*? Oh no, this really is a Temporal Distort… Wait, no, Andrew and Nicola Taylor actually converted *the entire army* from a whole host of Citadel kits for use in a Warhammer 40,000 doubles tournament at Warhammer World and played using the Codex: Witch Hunters rules.

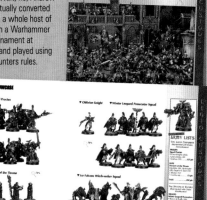

T'AU EMPIRE

Planning your next army? Wondering what to collect next? Or maybe even thinking about your very first army. Here's our regular guide to getting started with a new army or a new game, with top tips from those who know them best. This month, it's the T'au!

The T'au are an exciting proposition for any fan of Warhammer 40,000. Why? Because they're completely different to all the other factions out there in the galaxy. They're forward thinking and progressive, unlike the Imperium and the Aeldari and they seek to bring enlightenment to the galaxy, not see it burn like the servants of Chaos. On the battlefield the T'au are a force to be reckoned with, and they are known for packing a serious punch in the shooting phase – even the Imperial Guard will struggle to match them shot for shot. To complement their ferocious firepower, the T'au are also highly mobile, utilising anti-grav tanks and high-tech battlesuits to position their guns right where they need them ready to deliver the killing blow. Commanding a T'au army is much like conducting an orchestra – get all your units in the right place at the right time and the results will be magnificent. The best way to start a T'au army is with the Start Collecting! T'au set, which includes a unit of Fire Warriors, an Ethereal and a team of Crisis Battlesuits.

START COLLECTING! T'AU EMPIRE

"FIRE WARRIORS ARE THE MAINSTAY OF ANY T'AU ARMY IN MY OPINION," SAYS WARHAMMER COMMUNITY'S SARAH WALLEN. "THEY CAN PUT OUT A LOT OF FIREPOWER, THE MODELS ARE GREAT AND THEY COME WITH THE AWESOME DS8 DRONE TURRET."

"ETHEREALS ARE THE SPIRITUAL LEADERS OF THE T'AU EMPIRE," SAYS OUR WRITER DAN. "I OFTEN TAKE ONE IN MY ARMY AS THEY CAN REALLY BOOST THE FIREPOWER OF YOUR UNITS AND HELP THEM STAND THEIR GROUND WHEN TIMES GET TOUGH!"

XV8 CRISIS BATTLESUITS

"NO T'AU ARMY IS COMPLETE WITHOUT CRISIS BATTLESUITS," SAYS OUR PHOTOGRAPHER JONATHAN. "THEY ARE SUCH AN ICONIC UNIT AND THEY CAN BE EQUIPPED WITH LOADS OF DIFFERENT WEAPONS TO DEAL WITH ANY THREAT, BE IT INFANTRY OR TANKS."

ETHEREAL

FIRE WARRIORS

PATHFINDER TEAMS

MONT'KA

MONT'KA, OR THE KILLING BLOW, IS THE OFFENSIVE ASPECT OF T'AU WARFARE. KEY ENEMY UNITS SUCH AS COMMANDERS ARE IDENTIFIED AND MARKED, THEN ANNIHILATED WITH A PIN-POINT BATTLESUIT STRIKE.

KAUYON

THE KAUYON, OR PATIENT HUNTER, IS THE DEFENSIVE ASPECT OF T'AU WARFARE. THE ENEMY IS LURED INTO AN ALL-OUT ATTACK, THEN OUTMANOEUVRED, SURROUNDED AND DESTROYED BY T'AU FORCES.

"T'AU PATHFINDERS SET UP THE KILLING SHOTS, MARKING ENEMY TARGETS SO YOUR OTHER UNITS CAN OBLITERATE THEM." SAYS MATT, A VIOR'LA SEPT COMMANDER. "THEY KNOW THEY'LL PROBABLY DIE DOING IT, BUT IT'S ALL FOR THE GREATER GOOD."

XV8 CRISIS BATTLESUITS

XV95 GHOSTKEEL BATTLESUITS

"BATTLESUIT COMMANDERS ARE THE EPITOME OF THE MONT'KA, DROPPING IN BEHIND ENEMY LINES TO DELIVER THE PERFECT KILL." SAYS MINIATURES DESIGNER MATT HOLLAND. "THEY HAVE POWERFUL GUNS AND KNOW HOW TO USE THEM!"

XV25 STEALTH BATTLESUITS

XV86 COLDSTAR T'AU COMMANDER

"GHOSTKEELS AND STEALTH TEAMS CAUSE HAVOC ON A BATTLEFIELD AND THEIR MANOEUVRABILITY AND STEALTH FIELDS SHOULD KEEP THEM SAFE FROM ENEMY FIRE," SAYS DAN. "THE GHOSTKEEL MODEL IS ALSO AWESOME TO BUILD!"

XV104 RIPTIDE BATTLESUITS

"THE PIRANHA WAS ONE OF THE FIRST T'AU UNITS I BOUGHT," SAYS SARAH. "IT TICKS ALL THE BOXES FOR ME - IT LOOKS COOL, IT'S FAST, IT HAS PLENTY OF GUNS (HOORAY FOR BURST CANNONS!) AND YOU CAN MAKE ZOOMING NOISES WHEN YOU MOVE IT."

"RIPTIDES ARE LIKE THE NOBLE KNIGHTS OF THE T'AU," SAYS DAN. "I USE THEM TO SPEARHEAD ASSAULTS AND TAKE ON THE ENEMY'S TOUGHEST UNITS - I CURRENTLY HAVE FOUR OF THEM IN MY COLLECTION. MY MOTTO: ALWAYS NOVACHARGE THEIR REACTORS."

TX4 PIRANHA

TWO ALIEN RACES FIGHT ALONGSIDE THE T'AU - THE KROOT AND THE VESPID. NOT ONLY DO THEY PROVIDE NEW TACTICAL OPTIONS IN YOUR GAMES, THEY ALSO PROVIDE NEW PAINTING CHALLENGES, AS THEY LOOK VERY DIFFERENT TO THE REST OF THE ARMY.

"STORMSURGES ARE A TERRIFYING PROSPECT FOR MOST OPPONENTS AS THEY JUST HAVE SO MANY GUNS," SAYS JONATHAN. "PLACED IN THE CENTRE OF YOUR BATTLELINE, THEY CAN DEFEND YOUR ARMY WHILE DESTROYING THE ENEMY'S FROM AFAR."

"I PLAN TO HAVE AT LEAST TWO HAMMERHEAD GUNSHIPS IN MY ARMY ONE DAY," SAYS JONATHAN. "I'M GOING TO UPGRADE ONE OF THEM WITH LONGSTRIKE, TOO, MAKING THEM EVEN MORE ACCURATE. GIVE THEM SMART MISSILES FOR EXTRA PUNCH."

VESPID STINGWINGS

HAMMERHEAD GUNSHIP

KROOT CARNIVORES

KV128 STORMSURGE

SEE THE WHOLE RANGE AT: GAMES-WORKSHOP.COM

BIRTH OF THE IDONETH

Designers' Notes is the part of the magazine where we chat to the miniatures designers about their work. This month, Design Studio luminaries Ben Jefferson and Seb Perbet rise from the murky depths of the Studio to tell us more about the Idoneth Deepkin.

SEB PERBET & BEN JEFFERSON
Seb is well known for his work on the aelf ranges over the years. Working alongside Ben, he helped define the Idoneth Deepkin range you see today.

The Idoneth Deepkin are arguably one of the most unusual and fantastical armies to emerge from the Citadel Design Studio – for us in White Dwarf they're right up there with the Kharadron Overlords that came out just over a year ago. Of course, we wanted to know all about the new miniatures, so we caught up with two of the chaps that worked on the project – miniatures design manager Ben Jefferson and miniatures designer Seb Perbet. Here's what they had to say about bringing the Idoneth Deepkin to life.

WHAT MAKES AN AELF AN AELF?

Seb Perbet: Ever since Warhammer Age of Sigmar came out we've been coming up with ideas for what we could do with the aelves. There's so much scope for them it's crazy, with loads of opportunities to play on their culture, gods, obsessions and fears. There is always that lure of the three archetypes – High Elves, Dark Elves and Wood Elves – but we wanted to create something truly fantastical and otherworldy with this range. I came up with a load of concept designs for different aelves, looking for themes and patterns, aesthetics that would make for a cohesive, exciting army.

Ben Jefferson: There are lots of elements that make up a Warhammer aelf and understanding them was crucial to the birth of the Idoneth. Aelves are magical beings – they are attuned to nature, they are arrogant and aloof, they are selfish and, at times, cruel. They look down on other races with contempt more often than pity.

Seb: Then there are the physical aspects to take into consideration. Aelves are lithe, graceful and fast. They don't carry heavy or clunky equipment, their armour and weapons are extremely well

made and aesthetically pleasing – there's a degree of art to their wargear. And, of course, they have pointy ears – you can't forget that bit! But the faction background of an aelf also needs to be visible on the model – it needs to reflect their character. The Sylvaneth have aspects of nature about them, of life, growth and mysticism. The Daughters of Khaine are clearly more evil – they have blades on their armour and carry barbed weapons – they are visibly more aggressive and angry. So whatever we came up with this time also needed to have its own distinct identity.

THE FIRST STEPS ON THE PATH TO REBIRTH

Seb: I liked the idea of creating something tribal with the aelves, combining bare arms and torsos with tassels and lightweight armour – something that harked back to the very earliest days of the aelven race. Something primal, but still mystical and cultured that took them right back to their roots. Ben and I talked about the aelves' affinity with nature and that inspired the patterns that appear on their armour – particularly on the greaves of the Namarti and the Akhelian Guard – which I sculpted to look like waves. Or, rather, the shapes that waves make in the sand on a beach – that tidal ripple. So where the Sylvaneth were attuned to the nature of trees and growth and earth, these aelves would be attuned to water, seas and storms. ▶

EVOLUTION OF THE AELVES

Seb: The other aelf ranges – the Sylvaneth and Daughters of Khaine – had some strong influences on the Idoneth Deepkin. The Namarti Thralls and Reavers (designed by Maxime Corbeil and Christian Hardy, respectively) wear armoured belts that feature a gemstone in the middle, much like the Sylvaneth Tree-Revenants have a soul pod in their navels. But then the barbed collars and scars of the Namarti are more reminiscent of the Daughters of Khaine and their cruel nature. There will always be commonalities of design across the aelf ranges (it's those pointy ears again!), but the blind eyes of the Namarti and the hairless heads of the Idoneth faction as a whole really help set them apart from their kin.

Sylvaneth
Tree-Revenant

Idoneth Deepkin
Namarti Thrall

Daughters of Khaine
Blood Sister

Most of the Idoneth models have a degree of forward movement to them, just like a wave. As an army, the Namarti form the base of the wave, the Akhelians the body and the Leviadons and Eidolons the crest.

DESIGNERS' NOTES

THE ISHARANN AND AKHELIANS – LEADERS OF THE IDONETH DEEPKIN

The enclaves of the Idoneth are ruled over by the Isharann and the Akhelians – mages and warlords respectively. Most respected of all is Volturnos, High King of the Deeps.

"The Soulrender has the look of a slave-catcher," says Seb. "He's a barbaric-looking aelf with a brutal-looking weapon – his talúnhook is a visual metaphor for the dangerous task he has of capturing the souls of the departed. His rakerdart is his faithful hound, rounding up prospective victims."

"The Tidecaster is your archetypal aelven wizard," says Seb. "She's the noblest looking of the lot – the closest to Teclis's vision of the Cythai. She has a lot of nautical imagery on her – the clamshell crest, the shell on her staff, the barnacles on her base and the water rune in her hand."

"The Soulscryer, on the other hand, doesn't look noble at all – he looks sinister and cruel, like an evil wizard," says Seb. "He's a navigator in one sense, but he's more like a living dowsing rod, always searching for souls. The leaf compass and wind chimes emphasise his mystical navigatory skills."

THE RUNE OF MATHLANN

Ben: Seb has worked on several aelf ranges over the years and helped define many of the major runes for the Dark Elves and Wood Elves (as they were once known) based on the original High Elf designs. The rune of Mathlann used by the Idoneth is an adaptation of Mathlann's original rune and features a crown, a trident topped by a whirlpool and a trio of waves flowing across the shaft of the trident. It features sharp edges and curved motifs, combining High Elf and Dark Elf rune aesthetics so that it is somewhere in between – a merging of thought processes and emotions.

▶ **Ben:** There was definitely the look of pirates and raiders about them even at this stage – they felt more barbaric than what we were used to with aelves. What was really interesting was that Seb had given them bare torsos and arms, these cruel-looking collars and then really neat robes. There was an interesting juxtaposition there.

Seb: The Idoneth look cruel but noble at the same time. You're meant to look at them and be undecided about their intentions. Their robes are all really neat and clean with no ragged edges – they're immaculate. Their armour is finely crafted, too, with smooth lines and curves. But then you look at their weapons and you can't decide if they're good guys any more. Many of their blades feature wave-crest motifs that look like hooks and barbs while the hilts of their swords are shaped like fish bones. For the most part they also have cruel faces and, of course, no hair, which is pretty unusual from what we've come to know of aelves over the years. Initially I thought a shaved head would be better for swimming – a practical reason – but actually it helps make them look a lot more sinister. They're an interesting mix of elegance and spitefulness. Overall, I think the Idoneth physically look a bit more evil than good, which is why I suggested to the 'Eavy Metal team to paint them in nautical blues and silvers to make them look more ambiguous.

Ben: Another important factor is that they're not covered in fish imagery or sea shells or scales – we wanted them to be quite austere, like they'd come to understand that their decadence led to their downfall. We saved most of the nautical imagery for their bases. Saying that, there are very few gemstones on the models either and no banners – they have totems and icons, which give

> ## "I wanted the Idoneth to look cruel but noble. You're meant to look at them and be undecided about their intentions."

off a more tribal feel. There's a simplicity to the Idoneth, but an aelven simplicity, which means they're still far grander than most humans!

THE SOUL STEALERS

Ben: A big part of the background for the aelves in Warhammer Age of Sigmar is that their souls are being rescued from the clutches of Slaanesh – in the case of the Idoneth they're being rescued by Teclis – so they can be born again. But what if, like Morathi and her children, the Idoneth Deepkin were tainted? We thought, wouldn't it be interesting if some of the Idoneth were hail ▶

"Lotann is my favourite model in the range," says Ben. "I remember Seb coming up with the idea of this officious-looking statistician and we said it would be great if he had a minder. Seb decided on the Ochtar, an intelligent, multitasking creature to protect him."

"Volturnos is the most piratical looking of the Idoneth," says Seb. "He's got an eyepatch and a cutlass, but he still looks like a noble leader, with his billowing cape and the shell-like crest acting as a halo behind his head. His deepmare mount, like those of other Akhelian Kings, is also one of the few Idoneth creatures that isn't blinkered. This suggests that it has been tamed rather than magically broken in, showing Volturnos's mystical strength of character."

The Akhelians are the embodiment of raiding corsairs – nets, bottles and pouches slung across their Fangmora mounts. Their armour features more blades and spikes than that of the Namarti.

DESIGNERS' NOTES

▶ and hearty, but others were soul-tainted. And that's when we created the divide in the army between the different classes. On one hand there is the nobility – the Akhelians and the Isharann – whose souls were intact. On the other are the Namarti, whose souls were incomplete.

Seb: The idea of the Idoneth being soul-raiders came pretty naturally after that. Of course, if you're going on a raid, you need some fast-moving cavalry and that's where the Akhelians come in. I'd already come up with ideas for the Leviadon, Fangmora Eels and Allopex, which Alex Hedström, Ollie Norman and Samir Battistotti, respectively, ended up designing. We talked a lot about where and how the Idoneth would live and felt that a nomadic look was appropriate for them, that their war parties would often travel for long periods before getting to their destination. That's why the Akhelians have packs and pouches strapped to their saddles, plus ropes and nets, bottles, charters, maps and soul ledgers – they carry what's necessary for sustenance and capturing souls and little else. The sea creatures swimming around on their bases were a natural extension of their raiding nature, like the flotsam that a wave would naturally bring with it as it surges against the shore. They help scale the larger monsters, too, and add an extra level of narrative and depth to the army as a whole.

SUMMONING THE ETHERSEA

Ben: We often talked about the Idoneth bringing the spirit of the ocean with them into battle, which would include all the flora and fauna that live around them. There was no question for us how they did it – it was all down to aelven magic.

Seb: Aelves are the masters of magic and they can pretty much warp reality to be whatever they want it to be. If they want to convince a few fish

> ## "Are they flying in air or swimming in water? The point is, it's not meant to be immediately obvious..."

into believing they're still underwater, they will! They are meant to be confusing and make you question what you are seeing – just like an enemy warrior would on the battlefield. There are bits of coral and small fish in most of the kits (see opposite) that reinforce the supernatural sea that surrounds the Idoneth as they fight. But are the creatures real or an apparition? Are they flying in air or swimming in water? The point is, it's not meant to be immediately obvious – it's meant to be beyond our understanding as mere humans. ▶

A Namarti will die if they do not have a soul to sustain them. Lotann constantly balances the soul ledgers to ensure that the number of souls captured outweighs those that are lost.

CREATURES OF THE DEEPS

Many and varied are the creatures that dwell beneath the surfaces of the seas and oceans of the realms. Here are just a few of these wondrous beasts, from the half-tamed Fangmora Eel to the magical apparition that is the deadly rakerdart.

Fangmora Eel ridden by Akhelian Morsarr Guard

Deepmare ridden by an Akhelian King

Allopex with Akhelian riders

Ochtar

Dritchleech

Phantasmaray

Hippocampus

Engorger Fish

Scryfish Shoal

Stormfish Shoal

Malefic Screet

Rakerdart

Juvenile Quadtare

Direbrine Angler

Snapping Brón

Whorlscuttler

Glaubfin

DESIGNERS' NOTES

THE LEVIADON, ARMOURED COLOSSUS OF THE DEEPS

There are few undersea creatures as feared as the Leviadon. Fierce, stubborn and heavily armoured, it can crush entire regiments of enemy warriors with its bladed fins and fang-lined maw.

The Leviadon is blinkered (1), part of the binding ritual that prevents it turning on its Akhelian crew.

Ma'harr beast-rider (2). The Ma'harr is a high-ranking member of the Akhelian Corps and wears robes as a sign of his status. A Ma'harr is often heavily scarred, having had as many close encounters with vicious sea beasts as enemy warriors.

Akhelian harpoon gunner (3) — usually one of the youngest (and therefore least experienced) members of the Akhelian Corps, having just passed their Trial of Endurance.

Razorshell harpoon racks (4).

Void Drum (5). A rhythm beaten on this drum distorts the ethersea around the Leviadon, confusing the aim of enemy archers and gunners.

The Void Drummer (6) — one of the Namarti half-souls.

The rune of Mathlann, god of the sea (7).

Tribal sea-fronds (8).

The fighting platform (9). Superstructure made by Chorralus architects and builders. From the side you can see the wave pattern on the battlements — a pattern that's repeated on Idoneth armour.

Nets for capturing live victims (10) for later soul extraction.

Bladed tail (11) for slashing through enemies below.

The barnacle-encrusted shell of the Leviadon (12). Even the strongest enemies will struggle to penetrate it.

Razorshell Harpoon launcher (13).

The Leviadon's fins are covered in razor-sharp blades (14). Even a passing swipe could be a decapitating one.

Whirlpool rune of the deeps (15).

Crew packs and pouches (16).

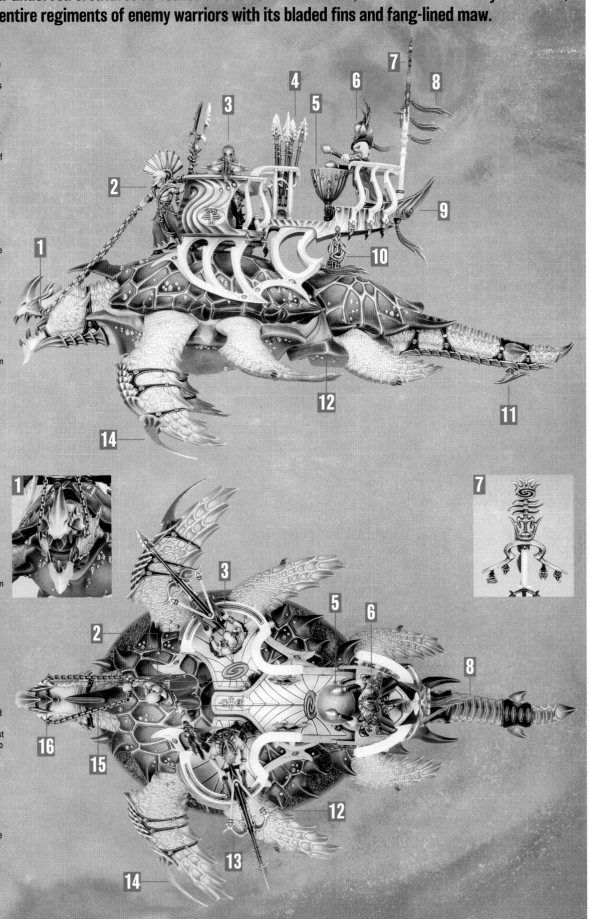

The Eidolon's base shows an underwater scene filled with fish and sea creatures, yet it's being rained on by his cloak – another great example of the mystical illusions that surround the Idoneth.

THE SPIRIT OF MATHLANN

Ben: The Eidolons are probably the most unusual aspect of the army because they're neither sea creature nor aelf – they're the spirit of a long-dead god, the collective memories, feelings and emotions of the Idoneth coalesced into a physical gestalt being. Mathlann, Lord of the Deeps was the obvious inspiration for this god-like being – who else would the Idoneth – the aelves of the

> "Mathlann could be benevolent, giving you sustenance and life. He could also be malevolent, turning on you in an instant."

sea – remember with such reverence? Mathlann could be benevolent, giving you sustenance and life. He could also be malevolent, turning on you in an instant – he was capricious, which was how we saw the Idoneth. They're neither good nor evil, but completely self-serving and insular.

Seb: And that's why there are two aspects to the Eidolons – the Aspect of the Sea the Aspect of the Storm. Both are more nautical in appearance than the rest of the army – with fish emblems on their shoulder guards and helm and fins and

BLIND TO THE DANGER
Ben: Something we've often talked about in Designers' Notes is the relationship between an aelf and their mount. High Elves and Wood Elves traditionally had quite a symbiotic relationship with their mounts, rider and beast respecting each other, while the Dark Elves broke their mounts in painfully, torturing them if necessary. For the Idoneth, we wanted their mounts to be utterly ferocious but magically tamed, which is why they wear blinkers to bind them – their minds are enslaved to the riders, who guide them with their reigns and bridles.

scales on their armour. This is even more evident on the Aspect of the Sea. His sceptre is shaped like a clam and features gilded fish around the head. His trident features a golden squid. Then, of course, there's the giant crown behind his head that's reminiscent of a sail or a fish's fin. He is more noble-looking than any of the Idoneth, with a fair face and flowing hair. He represents the kind, giving nature of Mathlann – he is everything the Idoneth remember that was good about the sea god. The Aspect of the Storm is far crueler looking, his eyes covered by his helm, his sneering mouth visible beneath. His helm features a crown of spiked blades and his spear and crulhook (which even has a chain hanging from it) are both barbed and hooked, like the scales and teeth of a fierce undersea predator. There are fewer fish emblems on him and more whirlpools. He represents the cruelty, fury, anger and destructive potential of Mathlann.

For me, the Idoneth Deepkin are an army of contradictions. They look noble but spiteful. Their equipment is beautiful but deadly. Some of them look like wizards and lordly knights while others appear to be slaves. Fantastical sea creatures fly (or swim – you choose) through the air around them, defying logic. They're also mystical, unfathomable, tenacious and dangerous – everything a Warhammer aelf should be! **DH**

'EAVY METAL MASTERCLASS

The 'Eavy Metal team are rated amongst the greatest miniatures painters in the world, which makes them the perfect tutors for a painting masterclass. This month, Martin Peterson joins us to show how he applies markings to beasts and monsters.

PAINTING MARKINGS ON BEASTS AND MONSTERS

MARTIN PETERSON

Martin is the newest member (and third Swede!) to join the 'Eavy Metal team. A nine-time Golden Demon winner, Martin was more than happy to share his top tips and tricks on painting markings on monsters and supernatural beasties.

The worlds of Warhammer are full of wondrous beasts, terrifying creatures and truly alien monsters, from the star-faring Seraphon of the Mortal Realms to the extragalactic Tyranids of the 41st Millennium. For many hobbyists, painting such unusual creatures is reward enough, but there are times when you may want to push your painting to the next level. Here, 'Eavy Metal painter Martin Peterson tells us how you can go about adding patterns and markings to your monsters.

"Monsters, mystical beasts and alien creatures offer a lot of great painting opportunities," says Martin. "Firstly, you can paint them any colour you can imagine – they're fantastical creatures so a red Gryph-charger or a purple Manticore is entirely appropriate. Because they often have large open areas of smooth skin or carapace, monsters are also the perfect miniatures to paint patterns and markings on, just like those you see on real-life animals. By that I mean stripes, spots, mottling and even weirder effects. Check out the patterns on a discus fish if you want to see some truly impressive markings! Below you can see just a selection of different patterns that we've used on monsters over the years. Like the colour of the model, there are no rules as to how the pattern must look or what colour it must be – you can have great fun coming up with incredible designs for your beasts. As with any model, the end result should look believable and be achievable – if you apply that logic to painting markings you can't go far wrong."

'EAVY METAL

The 'Eavy Metal team paint many of the miniatures that you see in our codexes and rulebooks, on posters and box fronts, on the Games Workshop website and in the pages of White Dwarf.

Since the early days of Games Workshop, the members of the 'Eavy Metal team have been at the forefront of miniatures painting, developing new techniques and colour schemes that can be seen on countless miniatures.

So great is the influence of the 'Eavy Metal team that many hobbyists see their work as the pinnacle of miniatures painting and seek to emulate their style on their own miniatures. Of course, painting this way requires a great deal of practice, time and dedication, and it's not going to be to everyone's taste or skill level – it would certainly take a very long time to paint a whole army the 'Eavy Metal way!

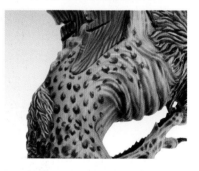

A LITTLE PRACTICAL THINKING

"Before you paint any beast or monster you might want to consider what colours will work best alongside your army's colour scheme," says Martin. "Imagine if the Lord-Aquilor's Gryph-charger (to the right) was yellow – it would be too similar to his gold armour. The same basic colour theory needs to apply to the markings you choose to paint on the model – they need to work both with the colour of the monster's skin or carapace and with the rest of the model. The easiest way to achieve this is to use a variation of the beast's skin tone. The Lord-Aquilor's steed is a great example of this, as is the Gyrinx on the opposite page (second row on the left). You also need a pattern that won't confuse the shape or outline of the model. Some real-life creatures wear camouflage to baffle predators. Not only is this really hard to paint, it often looks terrible on a tiny miniature, confusing the lines and details of the model. Go bold and clear with your markings and they will look much better for it!

"For this masterclass, I painted one of the new Fangmora Eels from the Idoneth Deepkin range, inspired by the Namarti Reavers that I painted for the Briomdar Enclave (*you can see them on page 66 of the* Idoneth *battletome. – Ed*) – I thought the colour scheme would work well on an Akhelian Guard. You can see how I painted it over the page."

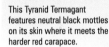

The pattern on the Lord-Aquilor's Gryph-charger mount has been arranged to look like a hexagonal grid that fades into the lighter skin on the beast's legs. Martin does something similar on his Fangmora Eel over the page. Note how the pattern has been applied to the large open space on the flank of the model and not to its forelimbs where the pattern could confuse the details on the model.

This Seraphon Bastiladon features a yellow mottled effect on its green carapace. When green objects become old and worn, their colour often fades to yellow – a perfect effect for a creature that regularly smashes itself into things! It's also a subtle way of applying natural camouflage to a model while also adding areas of interest and colour to its otherwise flat carapace.

This Tyranid Termagant features neutral black mottles on its skin where it meets the harder red carapace.

The patterns on this Tyranid Warrior appear on the edge of its carapace in colours that match both carapace and skin.

PAINTING THE SKIN

After undercoating the Fangmora Eel with Corax White spray, Martin blocked in the areas that would be painted a darker colour with Abaddon Black. He then set to work on the skin. "I painted the skin with a basecoat of Krieg Khaki (1)," says Martin. "It's much easier painting a light colour like this over a white undercoat. I then applied several thin glazes of Ogryn Camo over the Khaki (2), applying it only to the upper half of the eel (many creatures are darker on top and lighter underneath). With this stage, the glaze needs to be thin like a wash, but you don't need much paint on the brush (3) or it will run everywhere. The aim is to get a smooth colour transition vertically up the model. I then used the same technique to apply Elysian Green to the very top of the eel's skin near the fin (4).

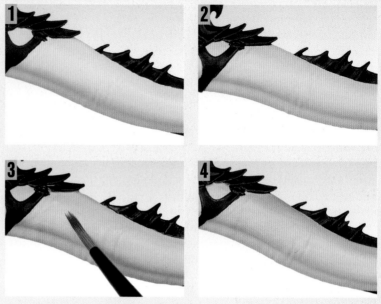

APPLYING THE MARKINGS

Having achieved a smooth colour gradient across the eel's skin, Martin turned his attention to applying his chosen markings.

"I did a lot of research into markings on different animals," says Martin. "I eventually settled on one that looked a bit like a tiger stripe, but green. I wanted the pattern to be really visible on the top half of the eel's body where the skin was darker and have it fading down into the lighter underbelly and towards the head and tail. Painting a pattern on a model's face is not only quite difficult, but also confuses a focal part of the miniature – better to save the markings for a more open part of the model.

"I started by applying a thin wavy line of Krieg Khaki down the eel's body (1). I watered the paint down a little for this – not as thin as the glazes I used earlier, but enough that if I messed it up I could paint over it more easily! Once the first vertical line was on the model, I applied several more lines parallel to it, with some of them splitting or becoming thicker or turning into loops. The goal is to make the markings look irregular, but still neat, with the lines fading into the belly underneath. I then applied thicker lines of Krieg Khaki over the first layer to further define the markings (2 and 3). The last stage was neatening up a few of the lines that I felt were a little untidy (4). I used the same colours I used earlier for the skin– Krieg Khaki, Ogryn Camo and Elysian Green – to carefully neaten up a few spots. If you're doing this, remember to water your paints down like earlier – don't be tempted to apply them directly to the model or the corrections will be really visible."

TOP TIP
"Before you put brush to model, try drawing out your pattern first to see what it will look like," says Martin. "A great way to do this is to use the diagrams on the instruction guide included in the kit as a template. You can draw several designs over the pictures (like I have done here) and decide on the one you like most."

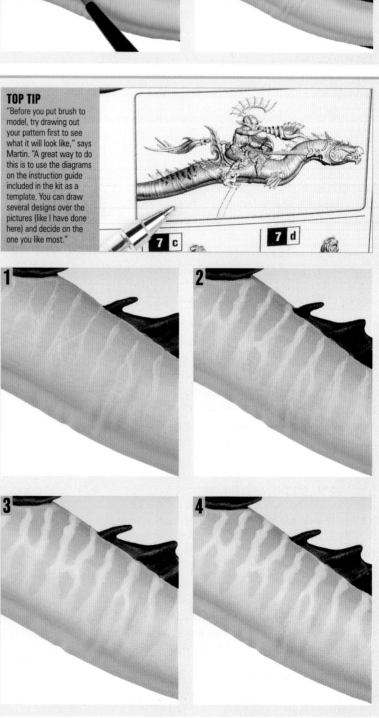

FINISHING THE SKIN

"The last stages are shades and highlights. It's important to paint these after the markings so that they apply to the pattern as well as the rest of the skin. I used a 50/50 mix of Loren Forest and Ogryn Camo to carefully paint in the folds in the eel's skin along the belly (1). I then used a 50/50 mix of Krieg Khaki and White Scar to highlight the edges of the folds and to create the faintest horizontal highlight along the length of the eel (2). It's a natural highlight point for the model that's likely to catch the light as you're painting it, showing you where to apply it."

PAINTING THE FINS

With the pattern now applied to the Fangmora Eel's body, Martin turned his attention to the fins along the eel's back. "The important thing to remember with the fins is that they are part of the same creature," says Martin. "You have to decide whether you're going to paint them to contrast with the skin – in which case you need to find a colour that won't overpower the pattern you've just painted – or be sympathetic to it. I opted for a colour scheme similar to the rest of the beast to show unity between the skin and the fin. I started with a basecoat of Castellan Green (1), then layered the fin with Deathworld Forest (2), a 50/50 mix of Deathworld Forest and Ogryn Camo (3) and then finally a layer of Krieg Khaki (4). These are all similar green and yellow tones to the rest of the Fangmora Eel."

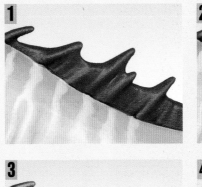

THE FINISHED MODEL

And here it is – Martin's finished Akhelian Guard on Fangmora Eel from the Briomdar Enclave. As you can see, the pattern that Martin chose to paint on it has been applied along the length of the model (except the head and the end of the tail) and the fin colour has been used along the length of the model. "The plan was to use natural colours on the eel, then really vibrant colours on the Akhelian Guard riding it to make her stand out," says Martin. "However, the colours across the whole model are analogous, with green as the primary colour and hues of blue and yellow to complement it. The eel tends towards yellow, for example, while the rider's clothing has a bluer tone to it – the contrast comes between the vibrancy of these colours. The rider's armour was painted in a slightly unusual way that's worth mentioning. I started with a basecoat of Kabalite Green mixed 50/50 with Ironbreaker. I then shaded it with Coelia Greenshade and Nuln Oil in a 50/50 mix and highlighted it with Stormhost Silver. It looks mystical and magical, contrasting well with the natural-looking eel." **DH**

SCIONS OF THE FURNACE

The Forge World of Ryza is home to some of the most ferocious warriors of the Adeptus Mechanicus. Red in cog and claw, they revel in close-quarter fighting. Here we chat to Jason Lee about his latest creation – a war convocation from the Furnace of Shackled Stars.

ere in the White Dwarf bunker, we love showing off great-looking armies. This month, we were delighted when Jason Lee got in touch to say that he'd just completed a new faction for the Imperial army he's been working on – an Adeptus Mechanicus force from the Forge World of Ryza. We expected to see a few units of Skitarii, some Onager Dunecrawlers and maybe an Imperial Knight. We certainly didn't expect this lot! We asked Jason to tell us more about his latest project.

"My Adeptus Mechanicus army is the next part in my grand plan to create one massive Imperial force for Warhammer 40,000," says Jason. "Over the last few years I've painted both Salamanders and Grey Knights (these I painted for Armies on Parade last year), representing the Space Marine contingents of my grand alliance. Now I've painted an Adeptus Mechanicus force to join them. All told, I now have around 21,000 points of units painted, but I'm aiming for 40,000." We can't possibly think why Jason picked that number… ▶

JASON LEE

Jason Lee is what many of us would call a painting machine. He paints large, high-quality armies at an astonishing speed, as you can see right here. In fact, he's already working on his next project. His brushes were hoping for a holiday, too.

Above: The Skitarii of Ryza are known for being fierce combatants, having fought off two massive Ork invasions before the coming of the Great Rift. As such, Jason invested in a Secutarii Hoplite conversion pack from Forge World to give his Skitarii a bit more punch (and stab) in close combat.

Below: Jason has painted four units of Kataphron Servitors for his army – two each of Breachers and Destroyers. "I do love the Kataphrons, but the Destroyers armed with plasma culverins do have a habit of blowing themselves up. I guess it's my own fault for supercharging them all the time. The carnage is worth it, though."

THE FURNACE OF SHACKLED STARS

So what made Jason pick the Forge World of Ryza as the homeworld for his Skitarii legion? "Really, it was all about the colour scheme," says Jason. "I liked the orange and white colours of Ryza, but I wanted to swap them around so the white was more dominant with orange as the spot colour instead, kind of like Forge World Metalica, but replacing the red with orange. Chris Bilewicz actually did this with his Imperial Guard and Adeptus Mechanicus force for Armies on Parade a couple of years ago and I thought it looked really great – basically, I copied his idea! Also, Dan in White Dwarf (*who, me?* – D*an*) painted a Skaven army with orange armour for Armies on Parade and they really caught my eye. It's a colour that doesn't get seen that often on armies, but can be really striking, so I thought I would give it a go. They would also stand out from my Grey Knights and Salamanders on the battlefield, helping identify them as a different part of the force. The only thing I kept the same on all three armies are the bases – they're all painted to look like a lava field with igneous rocks jutting out from molten lava beneath them."

THE MOTIVE FORCE

We asked Jason how long it took him to paint his army and how he kept himself motivated to complete it. "It took about half a year, I think, in between other projects," says Jason. "Once I get an idea in my head, I just get on with it and keep working at it until it's completed. I find there is a huge sense of accomplishment when you paint an army of this size and I kind of use that as my motivation – I know how good it feels to get a project like this done. A few people I know just buy more and more models until they end up with a huge, but pure sprue-grey, army. Painting that many models can be really intimidating – it's

FORGE WORLD RYZA

Ryza, also known as the Furnace of Shackled Stars, sits to the galactic east of Mars in the Ultima Segmentum. Having fought off the Ork invasions of Waaagh! Grax and Waaagh! Rarguts, the forge world has become entirely militarised. This is fortunate, for when the Noctis Aeterna descended, the Ryzans were more than prepared.

a psychological barrier – so I tend to build a few squads, normally around 30 models or so, and undercoat them all at the same time. Then I spray, airbrush or paint on the base colours of all of them. Once that stage is done, I focus on five to 10 models and get them all finished. Only then will I start on the next batch.

"I tend to focus on areas of an army in one go, rather than switching between different unit types," continues Jason. "I might spend two months painting infantry, then the next couple painting vehicles. I actually painted the Knights first in this force, followed by the Skitarii and the Kataphrons, then the seven Onagers."

AN ECONOMICAL APPLICATION OF PAINT

But is there a secret to Jason's painting – how does he complete armies so quickly? "It's all about being economical," explains Jason. "As I mentioned before, I apply all the basecoats first, which saves a lot of time. Then I spray all the models I'm working on with thinned down 'Ardcoat using an airbrush. I find this stage really important, because the next stage is a wash of Agrax Earthshade. I don't want the wash to stain the whole model and applying it only to the recesses would take quite some time. The layer of 'Ardcoat makes the surfaces of the model smoother and less adhesive, forcing the wash to

congregate in the recesses naturally. Like I say, it's a timesaver. Not everyone will go to these lengths, but once you've painted 50 Skitarii this way, the process becomes very quick and easy – its all about practice and feeling comfortable with the techniques you're using. The more you use them and the more you paint, the easier you'll find it to get an army finished.

> ### "I felt there was great contrast between the cold white robes and the hot orange lava, undersuits and burnished weapons."

"Once the washes are dry, I paint the white robes (you can see the colours Jason used over the page), then the metalwork and the orange areas. You'll notice the higher a model's rank, the more orange there is on the model. The Kataphrons only have orange unit markings on their track guards, for example, while the Skitarii wear orange undersuits. My Tech-Priest Dominus wears an orange robe to show how important he is. I also used Retributor Gold and a yellowy-orange wash on some weapons and wargear to give them a burnished feel. I felt there was great contrast between the cold white robes and the hot orange lava, undersuits and burnished weapons. ▶

FIELDS OF FIRE

All of Jason's models have lava bases that match those of his Grey Knights and Salamanders. The rock formations on the bases were built up using bits of a cork notice board with the edges roughed up to look more like rock. The bubbles in the lava were made with balls of Green Stuff cut in half and stuck in place. Jason then airbrushed the colours onto the bases.

CONVERSION CORNER

Jason: I love converting models – it's a great way to make each of them unique and give them their own personality. I also find converting great fun – altering a model enough to make it different but not lose its identity is quite a challenge. Imperial Knights are great kits to convert – I repositioned the legs on most of mine to give them more aggressive stances, and I gave a few of them different weapon systems to add a bit of variety. I try to build them to match the rules, but for me the look of the model is more important.

This Knight's head (1) has been converted using the targeter from a Land Raider's Lascannons. Jason cut it to shape, glued it in place, then used Green Stuff to fill in the gaps.

With seven Onager Dunecrawlers in his collection, Jason had a few Icarus arrays spare. He stuck them under the Knight's carapace (2) to represent an ironstorm rocket pod. Note how one of the missiles has been replaced by a heavy stubber.

After carefully cutting away the knee, Jason was able to reposition the Knight's leg to be raised up on a rock (3). Jason also remodelled the Knight's hip to get the angle right.

Jason converted this Knight Warden to be swinging a flaming censer taken from the Skaven Plague Furnace kit.

▶ You can see the gold most clearly on the Tech-Priest Dominus' axe head and the faceplates of the Secutarii Hoplites. I know they're not really elite warriors, but they do guard Titans, so I felt they should look a little more prestigious.

"The last stages of painting are the orange markings, the battle damage and dirt. The markings I apply over the white areas – armour or robes – to make them stand out. If I'm painting them on the hem of a robe or a straight edge, I start with a wide line of Troll Slayer Orange, then carefully paint in the cog teeth. I took a slightly different approach with the round cog icons. I drew a cog onto sticky back plastic then cut it out to make a stencil which I applied to the model and used as a template. This was especially handy for the Onagers and Knights. The battle damage was also really simple – a quick stippling of Rhinox Hide with a little piece of sponge.

NOBLE ALLIES OF RYZA

You can't have failed to notice the three Imperial Knights striding into battle alongside Jason's army, each of them painted in the white and orange livery of Ryza. "I like unity in my forces, so I just painted them to match the army," says Jason, laughing. "I've looked to see if there is a Knight Household on Ryza, but I can only find mention of the Legio Crucius – a Titan Legion. I guess whatever house they're from – I might even make up my own – changed their colours to honour the Forge World they're fighting with. Just like the rest of the army, I used orange as the spot colour for their heraldry. Like most people who paint an Imperial Knight, I kept the armour panels separate during assembly and painted the bare skeleton first before attaching the plates later. Painting the different heraldry markings was great fun – my advice is to always sketch out your design first before applying it to the model." ▶

PAINTING THE WARRIORS OF RYZA

When Jason told us how he painted his models, we thought it would be great to share the colours he used with you, just in case you wanted to paint your own Adeptus Mechanicus models the same way.

WHITE ARMOUR

Basecoat: Administratum Grey	Wash: Agrax Earthshade
Airbrush	M Shade
Layer: Administratum Grey & Ulthuan Grey	Layer: Ulthuan Grey
Airbrush	S Layer
Layer: 'Ardcoat	Layer: White Scar
Airbrush	XS Artificer Layer

ORANGE DETAILS

Basecoat: Troll Slayer Orange	Wash: Agrax Earthshade
S Base	M Shade
Layer: 'Ardcoat	Layer: Fire Dragon Bright
Airbrush	S Layer

METALWORK

Basecoat: Leadbelcher	Layer: Leadbelcher
M Base	S Layer
Layer: 'Ardcoat	Layer: Stormhost Silver
Airbrush	XS Artificer Layer
Wash: Agrax Earthshade	
M Shade	

GOLD DETAILS

Basecoat: Retributor Armour	Layer: Liberator Gold
S Base	S Layer
Layer: 'Ardcoat	Layer: Stormhost Silver
Airbrush	XS Artificer Layer
Wash: Agrax Earthshade	
M Shade	

BLUE LENSES

Basecoat: Sotek Green	Layer: Lothern Blue & White Scar
S Base	XS Artificer Layer
Layer: Temple Guard Blue	Layer: White Scar
S Layer	XS Artificer Layer
Layer: Lothern Blue	
XS Artificer Layer	

BATTLE DAMAGE

Stipple: Rhinox Hide
Piece of sponge

To make painting quicker, Jason applied all the white, metal and orange basecoats first, then airbrushed his models with 'Ardcoat. He then applied an Agrax Earthshade wash to all three colours at the same time.

This Knight Crusader has been converted by Jason to be striding forward into battle. Jason also converted the head to have extra targeters.

RYZA AT WAR

"The Adeptus Mechanicus can be a really brutal army on the tabletop," says Jason. "I haven't used the army a huge amount, but when I have they're devastating. Ryza's Forge World Dogma – Red in Cog and Claw – makes them really dangerous in combat, particularly the Sicarian Ruststalkers and Sydonian Dragoons. I've found my regular opponents tend to shoot them a lot now they've learned what they can do – they desperately don't want them to get in a charge! I also really love the Kataphrons, both as models and on the battlefield, but the Destroyers armed with plasma culverins do have a habit of blowing themselves up. I guess it's my own fault for supercharging them all the time – I need to remember to keep a Tech-Priest Dominus nearby to let them re-roll those 1s. The carnage is worth it regardless. Besides, the Ryzans can always build more servitors from the wreckage.

"I also played a game recently using only my Knights against my friend Pete's army of Knights. That was really interesting because we had pretty much the same weapons at our disposal – it was all down to positioning, tactics and stratagems. He won in the end, but it was a close game. It turns out Knights don't like getting hit by other Knights in close combat."

FUTURE ALLIES FOR THE GRAND ARMY OF THE IMPERIUM

But Jason is still not finished with his grand army of the Imperium. "I'm already working on some Adeptus Custodes and Sisters of Silence," says Jason. "Again, I'm batch-basecoating them all and then breaking them down into squads of five or so models to paint. I've also got to decide how I'm going to tackle the Imperial Guard side of the army – that will have to be a lot of models! And then I'm also eyeing up a Warlord Titan. I might have to save up for that one…" **DH**

WINNERS' CHALLENGE

For more than 30 years, Golden Demon has been the ultimate challenge for the very best painters of Citadel miniatures. But what, then, of a Champion of Champions? Join us, as we introduce the very first White Dwarf Golden Demon Winners' Challenge...

Golden Demon winners can rightly think of themselves as some of the best miniatures painters in the world. To celebrate this incredible standard of painting, we decided to introduce a new challenge, exclusively for those talented painters who've taken home a gold, silver or bronze Golden Demon statuette over the previous 12 months. The challenge is simple – paint a piece to fit on a 60mm round base, to a theme set by the White Dwarf team. This year the theme was a Warhammer Age of Sigmar one – the painter's choice of Order, Chaos, Death or Destruction. Here we bring you the first selection of stunning entries…

A QUESTION OF ALLEGIANCE BY NEIL HOLLIS

Neil Hollis won three awards, including the Slayer Sword at Golden Demon: Horus Heresy 2017, but he was more than ready to turn his hand to the Age of Sigmar. "I chose the theme of Chaos, inspired by a friend," says Neil. "My piece is a Chaos Lord deciding which Chaos God to favour. The gods have sent emissaries to sway his decision. He's standing on three books (Order, Death and Destruction) to emphasise his impending war."

STRANGE YET FAMILIAR

"The tricky bit was finding the familiars for each god and then getting them to fit on the base," says Neil.

"Luckily I found the Khorne one (1) from the Warhammer 40,000 Chaos Lord set – I just gave him legs. Half-way through painting, the Primarch Mortarion came out and the Nurgling on his base (2) fitted the bill perfectly!" The diminutive Tzeentch familiar (3) is from the Silver Tower game.

Neil's clever use of these familiars provides the narrative for the piece. "I was trying to convey a story between them – that the Nurgle and Tzeentch familiars are too concerned with facing off against each other while the Khorne familiar is offering his daemon weapon to the Lord for the upcoming battle. All the while the Skaven are sitting below the hierarchy, waiting for their chance to be held in proper regard as a true Chaos power…"

BETWEEN CHAOS AND ORDER BY KRISTIAN SIMONSEN

Kristian Simonsen won gold in the Warhammer Age of Sigmar Large Model category at Warhammer Fest 2017 with his Hell Pit Abomination. Kristian was one of several entrants in the Golden Demon Winners' Challenge to choose to make use of two different Grand Alliances in the shape of a duel.

"My chosen theme is the conflict between Chaos and Order. I see the two figures whirling around each other, very close, one on top of the other, locked in a battle to the death. The ground is lava on one side and lush, green and overgrown on the other, so it is not only the combatants, but the elements themselves that are fighting."

IN THE ENEMY'S GAZE

Kristian chose a Chaos Varanguard and a Stormcast Eternals Vanguard-Pallador as the combatants in his duel. The 'face' of the Varanguard (1) glows with the same lava effect as on the base. Kristian has used a technique called object source lighting to show the light of this fire illuminating the face of the Vanguard-Pallador (2), the combatants' gazes locked on each other. Kristian used this same technique to depict the fiery lava of the base lighting the whole piece.

1

2

GOLDEN DEMON

THE MAGNITUDE OF THE TASK BY BEN MACINTYRE

Ben MacIntyre won bronze in the Duel category at Golden Demon: Warhammer Age of Sigmar and chose another duel-type piece for his entry in the Winners' Challenge. "I chose a duel as I have always been a big fan of creating a narrative behind my armies, characters and Golden Demon entries," says Ben. "The interaction between the two works well with the menacing leer and imposing stature of the Tzaangor, and the determined (but pretty hesitant!) look on the Greatsword's face. The Greatsword is a nod back to an old Empire army I once had and played many a successful game with, so it was nice to revisit the scheme. The base was designed to add height to the Tzaangor and also increase the magnitude of the task facing the poor Greatsword.

"When it came to the painting, I wanted to take a bit of a new direction with this piece. I'm primarily a Khorne player, working mostly with darker colour palettes and a lot of grime and battlefield damage. I went for a traditional Tzeentch set of colours with a blue-grey skin tone and two very bright main colours to stand out against this. I added a really bright green in small key areas, such as the phials on the hip, to draw the eye around the piece."

> "The base was designed to add height to the Tzaangor and also increase the magnitude of the task facing the poor Greatsword."

DIFFERENTIATING PURPLES

Ben made use of a range of blues and purples – classic Tzeentch colours – on the Tzaangor (1 and 2) but by varying the brightness of these tones was still able to create vivid contrast. Some of these tones were also used on the Greatsword – such as the purple quarters of his clothing and the blue plume (3) – which ties the piece together while creating further contrast through the use of the yellow, applied only on the Greatsword.

1

2

3

THE HEROES' QUEST BY STEN FRÖDIN

Sten Frödin won gold in the Warhammer 40,000 Squad category at Warhammer Fest 2017 with his Genestealer Cultists. A fan of classic Warhammer and Warhammer 40,000 imagery, it's an idea Sten again picked up for his Winners' Challenge piece, on the theme of Order. "My idea was to build a small diorama inspired by the old Heroquest and Warhammer Quest games," he says. "I wanted to build a group of adventurers that look like they just stepped into a dungeon. The adventures, of course, had to be a Wizard, an Elf and a Dwarf." Long-time readers may recall that Sten appeared in White Dwarf back in 2015 discussing his love of the bold, clean 'Eavy Metal style of the 1990s. Sten has employed a similar palette on this piece which, like his choice of models, makes for a fitting homage to the classic archetypes.

A QUEST FOR PERFECTION

Sten chose an Ironbreaker model for his classic Dwarf adventurer (**1 and 2**), choosing a cool blue for his armour, and a contrasting deep red for the shield.

A Shadow Warrior provided the basis for Sten's Elf (**3**). He carefully converted the model to give it an adventurer's robes rather than the heavier scale armour of the original model. Sten painted the model's robes in a bright yellow, pairing it with a deep green on the cloak (**4**).

Sten built his Wizard (**5 and 6**) from a Genestealer Magos, removing the Cult symbols and adding a Wizard's head. Sten chose a rich, purplish red for the Wizard's robes. Between them, the three adventurers present a triad of primary colours – red, blue and yellow, standing out markedly from the blue-grey stone of the base.

1

3

5

2

4

6

GOLDEN DEMON

THE POWER OF THE WAAAGH! BY TIMOTHÉ BOSSARD

Timothé Bossard won silver at Golden Demon: Classic 2017 with his Avatar of Khaine. For the Winners' Challenge, he turned his attention to the forces of Destruction. "What attracted me to this miniature is its dynamism as well as its facial expression," says Timothé. "You can see the extreme concentration required to manifest such great power – or the stupidity that can animate such a being. I emphasised the power with some object source lighting around the Shaman's eyes and those on the head of his stick. I also wanted to try out brown shading and lightening of the skin, beyond the basic green. The pose and expression of this miniature is very inspiring and makes you want to paint multiple versions."

A BEAST IN BEAST'S CLOTHING

"I wanted to bring out the Shaman's bestial side, so naturally I opted for an animal skin pattern on his cloak (1). I planned to paint it like tiger skin, or at least in warm colours, but once I started painting the base (2) I realized that the combination of colours would drown the miniature. So, I opted for a zebra skin, to bring out the miniature while keeping warm shades of brown and beige. Surfaces like this are very interesting and allowed me to use some freehand."

1

2

YOUNG BLOODS

The Young Bloods category is an integral part of Golden Demon. Open to younger painters, a number of Young Bloods winners have gone on to win Golden Demon statuettes in many other categories. So, of course we knew it was vital to include the Young Bloods winners in this special Winners' Challenge!

NURGLING KEBAB BY DAIN KOOIJMAN

"It took a lot of time to make and paint this," says Dain. "The base is made of Green Stuff and cork and the slime threads are made of PVA glue. The slime is made of realistic water with a layer of Nurgle's Rot. I came up with the idea because my dad really likes the Nurgle army and I really like the Stormcast Eternals, so we thought we'd make a duel between them. We realised that we couldn't make too big a fight so we used some decorative Nurglings. It was really fun to make the Nurgling kebab and it also helped me improve my painting skills."

VARANGUARD BY JACK PITMAN-WALLACE

Jack Pitman-Wallace painted this Chaos Varanguard, mounting the model at a slight angle to emphasise the size and power of the daemonic steed as it rises up. Jack has painted a fiery red effect on the blade of the model's sword and echoed this on the front of the Varanguard's helm, for a powerful combination of black, gold and red.

NECROMANCER AND WIGHT BY JOSEPH WALKER

Joseph Walker converted and painted this Necromancer reanimating a Wight King, with Skeletons around both of them. Mounting the Necromancer on a rocky mound gives the figure height and, in combination with the brighter colours of the Necromancer, does a great job of drawing attention to him as the diorama's focal point.

GOLDEN DEMON

NO TROLLING BY KEV LAWRENCE

Kev Lawrence won bronze in the Diorama category at Golden Demon: Classic with a Middle-earth diorama. In fact, until now, Kev had only ever painted Middle-earth models. "I'd never actually painted a Warhammer model before," says Kev. "The funny thing is, I remember these Trolls from years ago, when I was a kid. I saw them in the window of a Games Workshop and they always stuck with me. But that was years and years before I ever got into painting, with *The Lord of the Rings*™ and, believe it or not, I never stepped outside of that. Until now. I really wanted to take part in the challenge and I knew it had to be these Trolls that I remembered from all those years ago." These Troggoths (formerly known as Stone Trolls) do indeed go back quite a way – in fact, as far as we can remember they were first released in 1993!

PAINTING UNDERWATER

Kev created an underwater effect for the base of his piece by carefully pouring clear resin into a mould – around the already painted lower parts of the diorama. "I've never done anything so nerve wracking!" he says.

Kev further added to the incredibly watery effect with some carefully drawn-out splashes, a leaping fish (2) and even a scratch-built shark (3) circling for any leftovers!

1

2

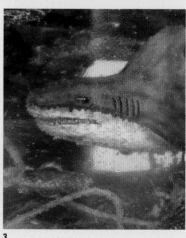

3

THE SUMMONER'S CHAMBER BY ANDY WARDLE

Golden Demon regular Andy Wardle won a number of awards at Golden Demon: Europe in 2016 to qualify for the Winners' Challenge. "I wanted to do something around the theme of Chaos, specifically the Silver Tower and Tzeentch," he says. "My idea was to have the Gaunt Summoner summoning an Ogroid Thaumaturge, rising from the floor of a chamber, surrounded by books." Andy has made use of object source lighting, using the purple of the glowing circle as a highlight on the legs of the Ogroid Thaumaturge to show light cast up from the floor, and the same magical energy rises from the book at the Gaunt Summoner's feet. **MK**

FORBIDDEN KNOWLEDGE

The many eyes of the Gaunt Summoner (1) create an unusual kind of focal point. By using a paler blue around those at the bottom, Andy manages to draw attention to the eyeless head.

Tweak (2), the putative Lord of Change, aids the Gaunt Summoner.

The Ogroid Thaumaturge's magical tattoos (3) glow with a purple reminiscent of that in the circle he has just been raised from.

1

2

3

THE WARRIORS OF THE
LAUGHING GOD

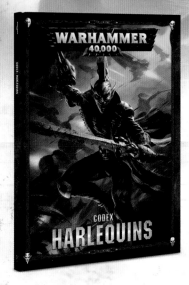

AELDARI WEBWAY GATE

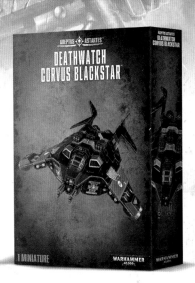

THE DEFENCE OF DREVARIS

Deep within the Damocles Gulf, the T'au Empire is expanding once more. In a bid to claim the industrial world of Drevaris, the sept worlds of Vior'la and D'yanoi deploy their forces. But to secure victory, they must first take on foes drawn from two Space Marine Chapters.

few months ago, miniatures designer Darren Latham (who also pops up in Hall of Fame on page 88) came to us with a request. He'd painted an army of Silver Skulls Space Marines and it had always been on his 'bucket list' to play in a White Dwarf Battle Report. How could we possibly refuse? Darren threw another idea into the mix. To get some tactics for his army, Darren had been chatting to Warhammer World studio manager James Karch a White Dwarf regular, who has a Sons of Guilliman army. As both Chapters are Ultramarines Successors, Darren suggested playing a four-player game with himself and James taking on two other players. That sounded like an even better idea, so we set off to find them some adversaries.

The first player to accept our challenge was miniatures designer Matt Holland, who – if you recall – joined us for a Warhammer 40,000 Battle Report last year with his T'au army. Matt had just painted a Stormsurge for his force, too, and had yet to use it in a game, so he was really keen to take on Darren and James. All we needed to do then was to find another T'au collector that could match the armies of the other three players. If only we could think of one…

In the end we just couldn't ignore Dan any more (his squeaking was becoming unbearable) so we nominated him as our second T'au player. The players were decided and so, too, was the mission – they would be fighting a Blitz!

DARREN LATHAM & JAMES KARCH
Darren and James both have a bit of a reputation for being competitive gamers. They both refuted this, then went for a team chat to discuss their tactics.

PREPARING FOR BATTLE

Darren: Before the game, myself and James got together to chat about our plans and how we were going to survive. A Blitz mission will be especially gruelling for us as the Space Marine defenders, with Dan and Matt constantly bringing on T'au reinforcements throughout the game. As our army gets smaller, theirs will likely stay the same size – we basically have to stay alive to the end of the game and keep them out of our deployment zones – not an easy task when the T'au are so fast. Fortunately, we all agreed that the first wave of T'au units could Manta Strike, but after that they would have to come in on foot. Having battlesuits continually appear in our deployment zone would have been horrible! To give our troops the best fighting chance possible, both myself and James upgraded our Primaris Captains to Chapter Masters using the Chapter Master stratagem. It's costly at three Command Points, but it can make a massive difference to the firepower of a Space Marine army.

Dan: Matt and I chatted a lot about what units to use in this game. Matt wanted to field his new Stormsurge and both his Riptides, and found that between them they came to almost 50 power – two thirds of his force! He'd also painted a load of Drones, most of them armed with markerlights to increase the accuracy of his army's firepower. To complement Matt's 'Big Suits Only' policy, I picked a more rounded army of infantry, Crisis Battlesuits, a Riptide and a Ghostkeel. Our plan was to distract the enemy with Riptides and battlesuits coming in from Manta Strikes, then use our other units to sneak up on the Space Marines, get into their trenches and score us some victory points. I also picked a Tidewall Shieldline for my Fire Warrior Strike Team to float into battle on. I've found that a moving fortification tends to confuse my opponents quite a lot and I hoped James and Darren wouldn't quite know how to deal with it. Only time would tell if our plan of attack would work.

MATT HOLLAND & DAN HARDEN
Matt is a keen tactician and loves to get the most out of his units. Dan tends to make unexpected tactical decisions that he feels are heroic. We're not so sure…

CRUCIBLE OF WAR: BLITZ
You can find the full rules for the Blitz mission on page 202 of the Warhammer 40,000 book. Rather than use counters for Concealed Deployment, though, we put up a screen across the board so we could set up our armies simultaneously, but sneakily!

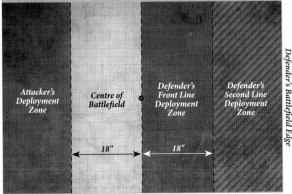

Attacker's Battlefield Edge

Attacker's Deployment Zone

Centre of Battlefield

Defender's Front Line Deployment Zone

Defender's Second Line Deployment Zone

Defender's Battlefield Edge

18"   18"

THE SCIONS OF THE ULTRAMARINES

POWER LEVEL: 154

SONS OF GUILLIMAN BATTALION DETACHMENT

HQ

1 – Chapter Master Ansellus
Primaris Captain with stalker bolt rifle, power sword and the Sanctic Halo (6)

2 – Lieutenant
Primaris Lieutenant with power sword (5)

TROOPS

3 – Battleline Squad 4
5 Intercessors with bolt rifles (5)

4 – Battleline Squad 5
10 Intercessors with bolt rifles, two auxiliary grenade launchers and Sergeant with power sword (10)

5 – Battleline Squad 6
5 Intercessors with bolt rifles (5)

ELITES

6 – Close Support Squad 9
5 Reivers with grav chutes (5)

7 – Ancient
Primaris Ancient (5)

8 – Oriax
Redemptor Dreadnought with heavy onslaught gatling cannon, onslaught gatling cannon, storm bolters and Icarus rocket pod (10)

FAST ATTACK

9 – Close Support Squad 7
3 Inceptors with assault bolters (10)

HEAVY SUPPORT

10 – Fire Support Squad 10
5 Hellblasters with plasma incinerators (8)

11 – Fire Support Squad 11
5 Hellblasters with plasma incinerators (8)

TOTAL POWER: 77

SILVER SKULLS BATTALION DETACHMENT

HQ

12 – Chapter Master Argentus
Primaris Captain with stalker bolt rifle, power sword and the Armour Indomitus (6)

13 – Lieutenant
Primaris Lieutenant with power sword (5)

TROOPS

14 – Battleline Squad 1
5 Intercessors with stalker bolt rifles, auxiliary grenade launcher and Sergeant with power sword (5)

15 – Battleline Squad 2
5 Intercessors with bolt rifles and Sergeant with power sword (5)

16 – Battleline Squad 3
5 Intercessors with bolt rifles and Sergeant with power sword (5)

ELITES

17 – Close Support Squad 16
5 Reivers with grav chutes (5)

18 – Lazarius
Redemptor Dreadnought with fragstorm grenade launchers, heavy flamer, Icarus rocket pod and macro plasma incinerator (10)

19 – Alenso
Venerable Dreadnought with twin lascannon, dreadnought combat weapon and heavy flamer (8)

FAST ATTACK

20 – Close Support Squad 8
3 Inceptors with assault bolters (10)

HEAVY SUPPORT

21 – Fire Support Squad 10
5 Hellblasters with plasma incinerators (8)

FLYERS

22 – Stormhawk Interceptor
Stormhawk Interceptor with two assault cannons, las-talon and typhoon missile launcher (10)

TOTAL POWER: 77

NOTES

Warlord Traits
James: Adept of the Codex
Darren: Storm of Fire

Chapter Tactics
James: Ultramarines
Darren: Ultramarines

Command Points
James: 6
Darren: 6

THE LIBERATORS OF DREVARIS

POWER LEVEL: 152

D'YANOI SEPT BATTALION DETACHMENT

HQ
1 – Commander Novastorm
Commander in XV85 Enforcer Armour with two fusion blasters and shield generator (7)

2 – Ethereal Aun'Chau
Ethereal on hover drone (3)

TROOPS
3 – Breacher Team Tores'kion
5 Fire Warriors (2)

4 – Breacher Team Fio'lan
5 Fire Warriors (2)

5 – Strike Team Shan'to
10 Fire Warriors with DS8 Tactical Support Turret (4)

ELITES
6 – Shas'vre D'yanor
Riptide with two plasma rifles, ion accelerator, target lock and two shielded missile drones (16)

7 – Crisis Team Rhi'un Li
3 Crisis Battlesuits with two plasma rifles, four burst cannons and four Gun Drones (14)

8 – Stealth Team Kai'to Aen
3 Stealth Suits with two burst cannons, fusion blaster and Marker Drone (7)

9 – Monat Es'loi
Ghostkeel Battlesuit with two fusion blasters, fusion collider and two Stealth Drones (10)

10 – Shas'la Ko'fes
Firesight Marksman (1)

HEAVY SUPPORT
11 – Drone Unit Zeta
3 Sniper Drones (3)

D'YANOI SEPT FORTIFICATION NETWORK
12 – Tidewall Asset 66
Tidewall Shieldline with Tidewall Defence Platform (7)

TOTAL POWER: 76

VIOR'LA SEPT OUTRIDER DETACHMENT

HQ
13 – Commander Brightsword
Commander in XV85 Enforcer Armour with four fusion blasters, two Marker Drones and Puretide Engram Neurochip (8)

FAST ATTACK
14 – Drone Unit Alpha
3 Shield Drones, 1 Gun Drone (2)

15 – Drone Unit Beta
2 Shield Drones, 2 Gun Drones (2)

16 – Drone Unit Gamma
8 Marker Drones (4)

17 – Sept Infiltrators Delta
5 Pathfinders (3)

18 – Sept Infiltrators Epsilon
5 Pathfinders (3)

TROOP TRANSPORTS
19 – Devilfish
Devilfish with two smart missile systems (6)

ELITES
20 – Firebrand
Riptide with two fusion blasters, heavy burst cannon, target lock and drone controller (14)

21 – Lightpath
Riptide with two smart missile systems, ion accelerator, target lock and advanced targeting system (14)

VIOR'LA SEPT SUPER-HEAVY DETACHMENT
22 – Vior'la's Fury
Stormsurge with pulse driver cannon, shield generator, velocity tracker, advanced targeting system (20)

TOTAL POWER: 76

NOTES
Warlord Traits
Dan: Exemplar of the Mont'ka
Matt: Precision of the Hunter

Sept Tenets
Dan: T'au
Matt: Vior'la

Command Points
Dan: 6
Matt: 4

BATTLE ROUND ONE: THE T'AU ASSAULT BEGINS

Having analysed the Space Marine forces, the T'au began their attack. Commanders Brightsword and Novastorm deployed from orbit, landing behind the Space Marines' lines, intent on causing as much disruption as possible. Meanwhile, the rest of the T'au forces attacked the Space Marines head on. Markerlights scoured the trenches, picking out the Hellblasters of the Sons of Guilliman and every available gun was brought to bear on them, blasting the Space Marines to atoms. The rest of the T'au advanced, attempting to cover ground as quickly as possible. An unexpected loss was the death of Monat Es'loi, the Ghostkeel pilot, who was blown to smithereens when his suit landed on a proximity mine. An unexpected gain,

CALCULATING VICTORY

In a Blitz mission, the defenders score one victory point for every enemy unit they destroy. The attackers add up their victory points at the end of the battle, scoring one point for each of their units behind the defenders' front line of deployment and two points for each unit behind the second line. The victory point tracker on each page shows how many points the T'au would be scoring at the end of each battle round.

however, was the destruction of the Stormhawk Interceptor, which was blasted from the sky by the Stormsurge's pulse driver cannon.

In retaliation, the Imperial Commanders brought their Inceptors and Reivers in behind the T'au, aiming to stall their advance. The reinforcements damaged one of the Vior'lan Riptides but did little else. Oriax the Redemptor Dreadnought also charged into the T'au lines and smashed its power fist into another Riptide, but its attacks just bounced off the suit's nova-charged shield. The Silver Skulls Dreadnoughts fared little better, the Redemptor barely wounding the D'yanoi Commander, the other scoring only light damage on the Stormsurge with its two lascannons.

The preliminary bombardment causes five wounds on James's Dreadnought (1).

All T'au units move forward, with both units of Breachers (2 and 3) advancing. The Stealth Team enters the trench (4).

The Ghostkeel (5) leaps over the first line of trenches and explodes as it lands on a proximity mine – one of the extra stratagems available to the defenders in a Blitz mission.

Both T'au Commanders, 14 Drones and a Crisis Team Manta Strike behind the Space Marine lines (6). The D'yanoi Commander does eight wounds to the Silver Skulls Dreadnought (7) with his fusion blasters.

Markerlights hit the Hellblasters (8), followed closely by devastating firepower. No Hellblasters survive.

The Stormsurge (9) kills two Intercessors (10) with its rockets, then blasts the Stormhawk (11) out of the sky with its pulse driver cannon.

11

12

17

16

6

7

15

11

14

4

5

"You're killing models you sculpted, Matt - do you hate them that much?"

Inceptors and Reivers arrive behind the T'au advance (12), shooting and then charging the Riptide Lightpath (13). They cause just three wounds on the battlesuit.

The Intercessors (10) fire on the T'au Breachers (2), wiping them out.

The Silver Skulls Hellblasters (14), Intercessors (15) and

Dreadnought barely wound the T'au Commander (16).

Oriax the Redemptor Dreadnought steps over the trench line, kills five Marker Drones with its

onslaught gatling cannon (17), then charges the Riptide Firebrand (18). Though several attacks slam home, the Riptide's nova-charged shield blocks them all.

T'AU ATTACKERS	10 - 2	SPACE MARINE DEFENDERS

BATTLE ROUND TWO: THE DEATH TOLL RISES

The T'au continued their advance, striking out at priority targets – namely the Redemptor Dreadnoughts. Oriax exploded when the Stormsurge fired a salvo of shots into it from its pulse driver cannon, while Lazarius took further punishment from Commander Novastorm. The rest of the T'au forces continued to advance on the first defence line, trading fire with the few remaining Intercessors still alive in the trenches, neither side causing much damage due to the sturdy defences they were hiding behind. The Vior'lan Riptides took on the Reivers that were still rampaging around their lines, killing the Sons of Guilliman but failing to catch the Silver Skulls, who charged into Firebrand to continue their reign of terror behind enemy lines.

Further back in the second line of defences, the Silver Skulls engaged the D'yanoi Crisis Team. Three Intercessors died in the firefight, but all three battlesuits were destroyed, the two surviving Hellblasters overcharging their guns to bring them down. Commander Novastorm once again escaped a round of shooting unscathed, though Brightsword was charged by several very angry Space Marine heroes, including Chapter Master Ansellus, a Primaris Ancient, Lieutenant and five Intercessors. The T'au Commander survived the encounter, but only because his Drones sacrificed themselves to let him live.

> **"I told you Redemptor Dreadnoughts always explode. Well, mine always does, anyway. Perhaps I should move it further away from my own units in our turn..."**

WHO BRINGS KNIVES TO A ROBOT FIGHT?

Matt: Space Marine Reivers are really nasty against pretty much everything in the game. Except, as it turns out, massive battlesuits with a 2+ save. Darren's unit did absolutely no damage to my Riptide in combat, which then ignited its jetpack, broke from combat and raced off towards the trenches. The poor Reivers continued to hound it, but clearly they needed something more than a knife to take it down.

The Ghostkeel returns as a reinforcement (1).

The D'yanoi forces move up on the trench line. The Breachers (2) lose three of their number to stalker rounds from the Silver Skulls Intercessors (3).

Oriax is lit up by markerlights and obliterated by the Stormsurge (4). The Dreadnought explodes, killing six Marker Drones, five Pathfinders and the Devilfish. It also causes five wounds on Firebrand (5).

Commander Novastorm (6) reduces Lazarius (7) to a single wound.

The Crisis Battlesuits shoot, then charge Darren's Intercessors (8) in a bid to stop them shooting. Darren then explains the Ultramarines Chapter Tactic to Dan, falls back with the Intercessors and shoots the Crisis team to bits.

Chapter Master Ansellus and his Chapter's heroes charge Commander Brightsword (9), who has to hide behind his Drones to survive the fight.

T'AU ATTACKERS   5 - 8   SPACE MARINE DEFENDERS

BATTLE ROUND THREE: WHEN HEROES FALL AND TRENCHES COLLIDE

A steady stream of T'au reinforcements continued to arrive, those units already engaged pressing home the attack on the now desperately outnumbered Space Marines. The Tidewall Shieldline made contact with the trench line and the Fire Warriors on board fired into the Space Marines, along with the Stormsurge and both Vior'lan Riptides. The Space Marines weathered the storm, however, shooting the last surviving Stealth Suit before leaping onto the Shieldline to fight the Fire Warriors, killing half before Aun'Chau intervened.

Nearby, Shas'vre D'yanor fired upon the Silver Skulls Venerable Dreadnought but barely scratched its paintwork. The Riptide took no

DEADLY AURAS

Dan: It didn't take myself and Matt long to figure out why both James and Darren had upgraded their Captains to Chapter Masters – their Rites of Battle ability means all units within 6" can re-roll to hit – much better than the regular re-rolling 1s. This, coupled with a Lieutenant's Tactical Precision aura, meant that the Silver Skulls and the Sons of Guilliman had an almost flawless hit and wound record with every attack.

damage in return, though, as lascannon shots glanced from the shield mounted on its arm. Commander Novastorm had a little more luck, finally killing the Redemptor Dreadnought and causing it to explode, killing several of the nearby Silver Skulls and wounding their Chapter Master. Enraged, Ansellus charged Novastorm and finally killed the T'au Commander as the rest of his units engaged the D'yanoi Riptide encroaching on their last line of defence. On the northern edge of the battlefield, Chapter Master Argentus also finally caught and killed Commander Brightsword. The Space Marines had scoured the T'au from behind their last line of defence, but they were now down to 24 battle-brothers and a Dreadnought. Would they be able to hold them off…?

T'au reinforcements continue to arrive (**1**).

The T'au Tidewall collides with the Imperial defence line (**2**) and three Space Marines are killed in

the ensuing firefight. They kill the nearby Stealth Suits, then leap onto the Tidewall to fight the Fire Warriors.

Commander Novastorm destroys Lazarius (**3**).

The Dreadnought explodes killing several Intercessors a Primaris Lieutenant and wounding Argentus. Argentus gets revenge by hacking apart the T'au Commander (**4**).

The Stormsurge kills two Sons of Guilliman Intercessors and three Reivers (**5**). The survivors shoot the last of the Pathfinders, then charge Firebrand, once again without success.

"It was like two battleships coming alongside each other and firing a broadside at point blank range into the enemy."

The D'yanoi Riptide **(6)** and Venerable Alenso **(7)** trade shots to no effect (and the surprise of all four players).

Brightsword flees from combat **(8)**, fires at Ansellus but does no damage when the Commander activates the Armour Indomitus. Ansellus then charges Brightsword once again **(9)** and finally kills him in combat.

The Silver Skulls defending the Imperial Bunker **(10)** target the Shas'vre D'yanor and cause several wounds on it, but most of the shots impact on its nova-charged shield.

Aun'Chau makes a heroic intervention to try and save the Fire Warriors on the defence line **(11)** but five of them are butchered by the Intercessors.

T'AU ATTACKERS	2 - 13	SPACE MARINE DEFENDERS

BATTLE ROUND FOUR: THE SPACE MARINES MAKE THEIR LAST STAND

The T'au were pushing home their attack on the Imperial lines, but the Imperial forces were punishing them for every inch of ground they took. The Fire Warriors – so confident behind their Tidewall only moments ago – fled from the Space Marine Intercessors that were attacking them and called for the T'au reinforcements to wipe them out. Most of the Space Marines died in the fusillade, but one escaped to chase Aun'Chau into no-man's land and into the sights of Venerable Alenso. The Dreadnought took careful aim and annihilated the T'au Ethereal with a pair of searing lascannon beams.

Across the battlefield on the landing pad, the Chapter Master of the Sons of Guilliman, his Lieutenant, Ancient and a lone surviving Sergeant weathered the storm of T'au fire, emerging wounded but still alive. Argentus of the Silver Skulls also remained in cover, his battle-brothers putting up furious resistance against the two Riptides bearing down on them. Only 17 battle-brothers and a damaged Venerable Dreadnought now stood against the T'au advance. Despite the piles of dead aliens around them, things were beginning to look grim for the Space Marines.

T'AU ATTACKERS	2 - 15	SPACE MARINE DEFENDERS

The Riptide Firebrand (1) uses the Automated Repair System stratagem to recover three wounds, moves into the first line of defence, then shoots everything it has at the Sons of Guilliman Intercessor Sergeant (2) but fails to kill him.

The Stormsurge (3) fires its entire complement of rockets at the same Sergeant, but only wounds him. It then fires its pulse driver cannon at the Reivers, killing both.

The Fire Warriors (4) and Ethereal flee from combat with the Intercessors, enabling the newly arrived T'au reinforcements to shoot them. The Intercessor Sergeant survives (5), leaps back into his own trench and bolters the last Breacher to death.

Shas'vre D'yanor leaps onto a pile of containers (6) and fires his ion accelerator at Venerable Alenso (7), causing three wounds. The Dreadnought kills Aun'Chau in return.

"I know he's a Sergeant, but I'm using my last command point to re-roll his save. He's taken over 30 hits, he's not dying now."

Lightpath, the Vior'lan Riptide (8), targets the last two Silver Skulls Intercessors in the trenches with a nova-charged ion accelerator, killing both in one colossal blast.

On the battlements of the Imperial Bunker (9), the Silver Skulls Intercessors and Hellblasters target the D'yanoi Riptide, but their shots are deflected by its shield.

Both Chapter Masters consider charging out to meet the enemy, but the incoming firepower is overwhelming. Argentus – already badly wounded – takes cover behind the

bunker (10) from where he can still boost the accuracy of his troops. Ansellus (11) remains on the landing platform ready to charge down and attack any T'au units that get too close.

A TRAGIC LOSS
Surrounded by the remains of a Ghostkeel and the dead bodies of his comrades, Shas'ui Fio'lan was having a terrible battle. Hiding behind an armoured container, he thought he was safe. He was killed by a single shot from James's last Intercessor.

BATTLE ROUND FIVE: FOR THE EMPEROR, HOLD THE LINE!

With the Space Marines falling back to their last lines of defence, the T'au advanced swiftly into the trenches. The Intercessor Sergeant that had butchered so many Fire Warriors was finally brought down by the Stormsurge, the walking battleship unleashing its payload on the lone Space Marine.

Further into the Imperial lines, Firebrand targeted the Sons of Guilliman once more, finally killing the Sergeant that had survived for so long. The other heroes of the Chapter took cover as ion accelerator rounds from Lightpath exploded around them, then leaped down from the landing pad to fight the Riptide but, like the T'au Commander earlier in the battle, it proved deceptively hard to kill. Nearby, Shas'vre D'yanor fired into the Silver Skulls Intercessors around the bunker, obliterating one of their number as several others were killed by long-ranged T'au guns. The luck of Venerable Alenso also finally ran out as his armoured shell was blasted open by the second Ghostkeel.

Yet the T'au could not kill the last few Space Marines, who stubbornly held their ground against overwhelming odds. Taking stock of their losses, the T'au Commanders calculated that regrouping and launching a new attack would be a much better use of T'au lives. Jetpacks ignited as they retreated into the mist. The nine surviving Space Marines waited for them to return.

The T'au storm the defence lines once more (1).

Firebrand drops behind the second Imperial line of defence and is attacked by Ansellus (2), while D'yanor (3) leaps over the trenches to engage Argentus. Protected by a squad of Intercessors (4), the Chapter Master survives the Riptide's punishing firepower.

T'AU ATTACKERS	FINAL SCORE	SPACE MARINE DEFENDERS
	9 - 15	

THE POST-BATTLE DEBRIEF

As the smoke cleared and the T'au attack faltered, the Space Marines stood victorious in the ruins of Drevaris! Only nine Space Marines were still standing by the end of the battle and five of them were wounded. Here's what the four commanders had to say about their game.

James: That was utterly brutal! Who picked that mission, eh? (*It was Dan. – Ed*) I was so certain we were going to lose. Actually, I'm amazed we didn't because the T'au assault was relentless.

Darren: I blame my own dice rolls. Even with all my re-rolls I couldn't hit anything. And the Redemptor Dreadnought exploding amongst my own units was horrible. I must remember not to set it up surrounded by other units.

James: We did win, Darren – we beat the dirty aliens. The battle's over now, mate!

Darren: I know, it's just I haven't fought a mission like this before – or at least not in a long time – so I was totally unprepared for how battered our armies would get.

> **"There were so many dramatic moments in that battle where the Space Marines went above and beyond the call of duty."**

Dan: On the plus side, though, those Space Marines that survived are proper heroes. There were so many dramatic moments in that battle where the Space Marines went above and beyond the call of duty. I honestly have no idea how James's Intercessors survived for so long – they just would not die, even when the Stormsurge fired into them. And the fight in the trenches was epic, with the two units shooting each other at point-blank range.

Matt: I loved bringing down our Commanders behind your lines. It felt like a real T'au assault.

Darren: Yeah, we should have put some units at the back of the board to stop you doing that. A silly mistake from us, there. I think we deployed James's Hellblasters too far forward, too – you really punished us for that. I can't believe you shot my Stormhawk – I had plans for that.

Matt: Hellblasters really scare me! And I just knew you would aim the Stormhawk at my Stormsurge – I had to kill it. I was surprised our Riptides lasted so well, though – I really expected them to die early on.

Dan: Primaris Marines don't have that many heavy weapons, though – once we'd got rid of the Hellblasters they were really going to struggle taking down the bigger battlesuits.

James: We still won, though. And we'll beat you again next time, too! **DH**

THE SOUL SIPHON

Idoneth Deepkin of the Ionrach Enclave have been drawn to the Realm of Death by the screaming of tortured souls. Striking deep into the realm, they discover an arcane device that sends soul energy to Nagashizzar. But perhaps the captured souls can be stolen...

Maughan the Soulscryer closed his eyes and dived deep into the spirit world. It was like plunging into an icy stream, for there was no warmth in this barren realm where the dead ruled and the living suffered. The screams of tortured souls came to him through the murk, their wailing distorted by the bitterly cold ether that engulfed him. It was hard to navigate in Shyish with so much necromantic magic saturating the air, but Maughan could just about trace the spirit energy.

It took him across bleak lands and deserted villages to a river – a man-made river by the looks of it – that churned with bound souls. Maughan followed their wake upstream, ignoring their cries as his spirit essence glided by, past long-deserted cities to a vast stone monolith. Dark magic saturated the air around it, drawn to a brazier burning at its summit. Maughan had found what he was looking for. Yet it wasn't the soul siphon that terrified him, for something else blazed with such abominable energy that it obliterated all light around it. His spirit essence retreated hastily to his body and he emerged from the spirit world breathing hard. The air was cold and crisp, but not even slightly refreshing. It tasted of death.

"You have found the way?" said Volturnos, looking down on Maughan where he sat. The High King's one remaining eye shone in the darkness like a gemstone, hard and intent.

"I have," replied Maughan. He could taste ash in his mouth. "But the Great Necromancer knows we're here. He is waiting."

O ur second Battle Report this month is inspired by the war of souls that seems to be escalating between Nagash and the myriad races of the Mortal Realms. As the Supreme Lord of the Undead seeks to master the underworlds of Shyish and claim the souls that reside there for his own, the forces of Order, Chaos and Destruction fight to stop him. Yet the Idoneth Deepkin have another motive for stopping Nagash claiming the souls of the dead – they want them for themselves. And that's what this Battle Report is all about. The Idoneth Deepkin have found one of Nagash's soul siphons deep within the realm of Shyish and are now trying to steal the souls bound within it for their own uses. Nagash, of course, is not keen on their plan and has set out to stop them.

For this game we used the Ritual scenario from the Warhammer Age of Sigmar book (page 162), but adapted it for our battlefield (which we featured in last month's Battleground article). The Idoneth Deepkin would have to get Maughan the Soulscryer to the soul siphon, where – aided by the other Isharann – he would begin the soul extraction ritual. Sam Pearson from the Design Studio would be taking command of the Idoneth Deepkin in their first Battle Report, while Martyn would be in command of Nagash's undead legions. They deployed their armies (see over the page) and prepared themselves for battle…

MARTYN LYON

Martyn loves a game of Warhammer Age of Sigmar and Nagash is one of his favourite Citadel miniatures of all time. You can probably see why he wanted to play in this battle.

SAM PEARSON

Sam is the newest member of the games development team and wrote the Duels of the Crystal Labyrinth minigame in this issue. He was very excited to fight his first Battle Report.

NAGASH'S LEGION OF UNDEATH

Martyn: My vision for an army of Death is rank upon rank of Skeletons, so I built my army around three big units of them. I also wanted to try out some of the new units in the Legions of Nagash book – particularly the Bloodseeker Palanquin and Prince Vhordrai – which gave me the idea of fielding lots of Vampires to defend Nagash's soul siphon.

THE GRAND HOST OF NAGASH

THE FIRST COHORT (160)

1 – Nagash, Supreme Lord of the Undead
Additional Spells: Decrepify, Spectral Grasp, Vile Transference (800)

2 – The Eternity Wardens
4 Morghast Archai (440)

3 – The Osseous Guard
20 Skeleton Warriors with spears (160)

4 – The Bone Legion
20 Skeleton Warriors with spears (160)

5 – The Silent Reapers
20 Grave Guard with wight blades (320)

ADDITIONAL UNITS

6 – Prince Vhordrai
Additional Spell: Amaranthine Orb (480)

7 – Count Tavrojk
Vampire Lord
Additional Spell: Blades of Shyish (140)

8 – Countess Jaedla
Bloodseeker Palanquin
Additional Spell: Spirit Gale
Artefact: Deathforged Chain (320)

9 – The Knights of Blood Tower
5 Blood Knights (260)

10 – The Knights of Skull Keep
5 Blood Knights (260)

11 – Lord Karnova
Wight King
Artefact: Ossific Diadem (120)

12 – The Shrieking Maiden
Tomb Banshee (80)

13 – The Damned Souls
3 Spirit Hosts (120)

14 – The Cursed Souls
3 Spirit Hosts (120)

TOTAL: 3940

THE HIGH KING'S SOUL HUNTERS

Sam: I picked my army from the Studio collection, taking something of everything so I could get a feel for the new army. I organised most of the force into three Warscroll Battalions, giving me access to loads of interesting artefacts. Aside from winning the game, my main goal was to give Nagash a bad case of the Brain Barnacles.

IDONETH ARMY OF THE IONRACH ENCLAVE

ROYAL COUNCIL (140)
1 – Volturnos, High King of the Deeps (280)

2 – Shevari
Isharann Tidecaster
Artefact: Brain Barnacles
Additional Spell: Arcane Corrasion (100)

3 – Maughan
Isharann Soulscryer
Artefact: Cloud of Midnight (100)

AKHELIAN CORPS (100)
4 – The Voidbeast
Akhelian Leviadon (380)

5 – The First Sons of Príom
6 Akhelian Ishlaen Guard (280)

6 – The Deepdelve Cohort
3 Akhelian Morrsarr Guard (160)

7 – The Ethersea Marauders
3 Akhelian Allopexes (420)

NAMARTI CORPS (100)
8 – Yranae
Isharann Soulrender
Artefact: Dritchleech (100)

9 – First Namarti Motiae
10 Namarti Thralls (140)

10 – Second Namarti Motiae
20 Namarti Thralls (280)

11 – The Reavers of Aeloth
10 Namarti Reavers (140)

12 – The Silvertide Archers
10 Namarti Reavers (140)

ADDITIONAL UNITS
13 – Terror of Maithnar
Akhelian Leviadon (380)

14 – Eidolon of Mathlann, Aspect of the Storm (440)

15 – Lotann, Warden of the Soul Ledgers (100)

TOTAL: 3780

BATTLE ROUND ONE: KNOW THY ENEMY

Volturnos ordered the Idoneth advance, the Namarti forming the first wave of the assault followed by the Akhelians. Volturnos decided he would, for now, remain with the cadre of Isharann, watching over them until they began the soul extraction. Nearby, Maughan the Soulscryer was already incanting a ritual, swirling the air above the ethersea into a dizzying vortex that would bring any undead creatures in the sky crashing to the ground. The other Isharann supported him in his endeavour, empowering him with mystic energy.

On the other side of the river of souls, the Ethersea Marauders raced forward on their Allopex mounts, followed closely by the Terror of Maithnar. It looked like the Great Necromancer's forces may try to flank his own army's advance and Volturnos could not have that happen – the Idoneth could not afford a war of attrition.

THE RITUAL
For Sam to win the game, he would need to complete the ritual. To do this, he would need to get his Soulscryer to the soul siphon – in the following turn he could then begin the ritual. Every turn the Soulscryer was next to the souls siphon Sam could steal D6 souls from it. When he got to 20, he would win the game. To improve his chances, we agreed that Sam could add one to his dice roll for every Isharann hero within 3" of the Soulscryer each turn. Martyn would, of course, be aiming to kill the Soulscryer and his fellow Isharann.

Nagash seethed with rage at the temerity of the Idoneth Deepkin – they were trying to steal souls that rightfully belonged to him! Even worse, their aelven magic had caused the skies of Shyish to roil with ethereal energy, their mystical ethersea flowing dankly around his army and leaving his airborne servants utterly grounded. No matter, death would come to them sooner or later. Nagash ordered his undead minions forward, intending to surround the soul siphon with a wall of Skeleton Warriors. His Soulblight children, having scented blood, were desperate to engage the enemy and the Great Necromancer had no desire to stop them. He idly unshackled them from his will and the Blood Knights roared down the hill through the graveyards. Those to the north failed to reach the enemy, but those to the south put on an unexpected burst of speed that saw an entire unit of Reavers trampled beneath their hooves. First blood had been spilt.

As the attackers in this battle, Sam and the Idoneth Deepkin take the first turn.

The Soulscryer (1) casts Ritual of the Tempest, preventing undead units from flying until the next Idoneth hero phase.

Volturnos (2) uses the Give Them No Respite command ability to increase the movement of three Idoneth units. As a result, the Namarti Reavers (3) and Thralls (4) race forward alongside the Ishlaen Guard (5) in an attempt to cordon off the undead advance.

The Eidolon of Mathlann (6) holds the Idoneth north flank, while the Morrsarr Guard head south (7).

SOULS STOLEN
BATTLE ROUND ONE
0

THE RITUALISTS
Sam: I placed all my heroes close together so that they would be able to offer my Soulscryer as much help as possible, not only in completing the ritual, but also when casting Isharann rituals (I can cast one a turn and the Soulscryer is the best aelf for the job). I deployed Volturnos near the Isharann as I reckoned he would be needed later in the game to protect them from harm.

A TWO-FANGED ASSAULT

Martyn: I was in two minds over how to deal with Sam's forces. He had committed most of his models (including all of his heroes) to the northern side of the soul siphon. I was debating whether I should sweep my army around the southern end of it and attack him from the flank or whether I should meet him head on. In the end I decided on doing both. Nagash and the Morghasts herded two big units of Skeleton Warriors down through the graveyards, while Vhordrai led the Grave Guard in the flanking force. Sam's Ritual of the Tempest that stopped my units flying, though, was a real hindrance to my battle plan…

TIDES OF DEATH
The army special rule for the Idoneth Deepkin is called Tides of Death. It changes at the start of every battle round.

Low Tide: In this battle round, all units with the Tides of Death battle trait are treated as being in cover.

The trio of Akhelian Allopexes (8) fly next to the canal, ready to move to reinforce either flank. Despite their swift advance, the Idoneth are out of range with their shooting attacks and too far away to initiate any charges.

Nagash (9) uses his Supreme Lord of Death Command Ability to make his army immune to battleshock. His offensive spells are out of range at this point, but he casts Mystic Shield on the nearest Skeletons in case they get shot at in the next battle round.

The Grave Guard (10) run (albeit very slowly!) down the hill followed by the Spirit Hosts. Unable to fly due to the raging ethersea tempest, Prince Vhordrai (11) is trapped behind his own units and cannot move at all.

The Knights of Skull Keep (12) race down the graveyard on the north side of the soul siphon followed by the two units of Skeleton Warriors.

The Knights of Blood Tower (13) pull off a very long charge on the Namarti Reavers and kill nine of them. The last Reaver flees from their terrifying onslaught.

Martyn wins the roll-off for the second battle round and decides to take the first turn.

Still unable to fly and still out of range to use most of his spells, Nagash (1) has to content himself with casting Mystic Shield on the Skeleton Warriors at the head of the northern advance.

The Grave Guard (2) advance down the hill, while Prince Vhordrai shoves aside the Spirit Hosts (3) to get into a better position.

The Knights of Blood Tower smash into the Second Namarti Motiae on the southern board edge (4), killing 16 of them on the charge. The survivors kill one Blood Knight in return, then flee the battlefield. To Sam's frustration his Soulrender is unable to return dead Namarti to the battlefield at the end of the battleshock phase, because there is no unit for him to return them to! The Knights of Blood Tower are then charged by the trio of Akhelian Allopexes (5). The aelven riders kill one Vampire, while the Allopexes crunch through the other three Blood Knights with very little effort.

SOULS STOLEN
BATTLE ROUND TWO

0

BATTLE ROUND TWO: DEATH AMIDST THE GRAVEYARDS

The legions of undeath continued to shamble forward under Nagash's watchful gaze, the Grave Guard following the Blood Knights down into the barrows and the Skeleton phalanxes marching down into the graveyards. Once again, Nagash looked for a suitable foe to vent his rage upon, but none were close enough, the Idoneth wisely taking cover behind the soul siphon.

Meanwhile, the Blood Knights continued their devastating charges, the Knights of Blood Tower trampling clean through a huge unit of Namarti Thralls on the southern flank. The few surviving aelves ran for their lives in the face of such a gory onslaught. On the northern flank, the Soulblight Vampires had a tougher fight against the Idoneth cavalry, but none fell to the thrashing eels. Nagash watched the Idoneth closely – those mysterious aelves were plotting something…

FIGHTING WITH THE TIDE

Sam: To get the most out of your Idoneth Deepkin army you really want to plan your attacks around the Tides of Death. In the third battle round all your units strike first in combat, so it's worth trying to get lots of them into a fight in the second battle round. That way, even if your opponent goes first in the third battle round (and chooses not to charge any of your units) you will still get to make lots of attacks. You then fight first in your third turn before retreating in the fourth battle round. The tides can be tricky to master!

With the Blood Knights in the midst of his army, Volturnos ordered the Namarti and Akhelians to engage them and pull them from their mounts – they could not be allowed to survive. As the Ishlaen Guard and the Namarti Thralls surrounded the Vampires, Volturnos urged his deepmare steed forward, flying over the Vampires to crash into the Skeletons piling down the hill towards the Idoneth. The Eidolon of Mathlann flew into battle alongside him, flinging the bones of broken Skeletons about like driftwood. Volturnos risked a glance over his shoulder to see how his other flank was faring. As he watched, the Blood Knights that had killed so many Namarti were attacked by the Ethersea Marauders, the trio of Allopexes tearing the undead lords limb from limb in a brutal act of revenge. The Morrsarr Guard near them were equally vicious, almost wiping out the Grave Guard that were marching down the hill.

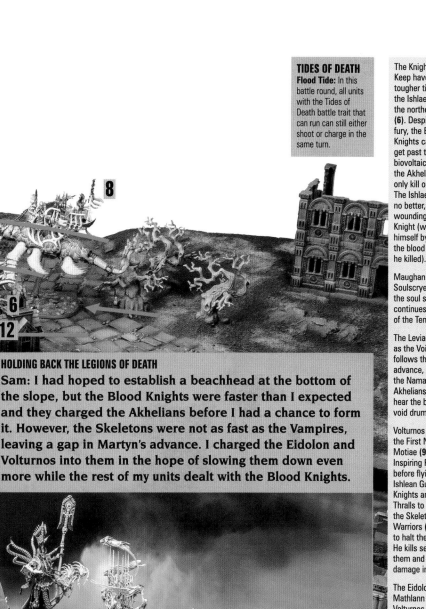

TIDES OF DEATH
Flood Tide: In this battle round, all units with the Tides of Death battle trait that can run can still either shoot or charge in the same turn.

The Knights of Skull Keep have a much tougher time against the Ishlaen Guard on the northern flank (6). Despite their fury, the Blood Knights can barely get past the biovoltaic barriers of the Akhelians and only kill one of them. The Ishlaen have it no better, barely wounding a Blood Knight (who heals himself by drinking the blood of the aelf he killed).

Maughan the Soulscryer reaches the soul siphon and continues the Ritual of the Tempest (7).

The Leviadon known as the Voidbeast (8) follows the Idoneth advance, ensuring all the Namarti and Akhelians nearby can hear the beat of its void drums.

Volturnos emboldens the First Namarti Motiae (9) with his Inspiring Presence before flying over the Ishlean Guard, Blood Knights and Namarti Thralls to charge into the Skeleton Warriors (10) in a bid to halt their advance. He kills seven of them and suffers no damage in return.

The Eidolon of Mathlann joins Volturnos amidst the graveyards, but charges into the other unit of Skeleton Warriors (11), killing 11, but suffering two wounds in return.

The Soulscryer uses Seeker of Souls on the Blood Knights, ensuring that the Namarti Thralls cannot fail to get into combat with them.

The Namarti Reavers (12) kill a Blood Knight with their Storm Fire ability before the Thralls and Ishlaen Guard wipe out the Vampires in combat.

On the southern flank, the Morrsarr Guard (13) charge the Grave Guard, killing four with a biovoltaic blast and another ten on the charge. The surviving Grave Guard do a single wound in return but do not crumble to dust thanks to Nagash's incredible mastery over the dead.

HOLDING BACK THE LEGIONS OF DEATH

Sam: I had hoped to establish a beachhead at the bottom of the slope, but the Blood Knights were faster than I expected and they charged the Akhelians before I had a chance to form it. However, the Skeletons were not as fast as the Vampires, leaving a gap in Martyn's advance. I charged the Eidolon and Volturnos into them in the hope of slowing them down even more while the rest of my units dealt with the Blood Knights.

BATTLE ROUND THREE: HIGH TIDE

Glaring down the hill into the graveyard, Nagash watched as Volturnos and the Eidolon of Mathlann smashed their way through his First Cohort. Furious, the Great Necromancer simply dragged more Skeletons from their graves to replace those he'd lost, then flung them to one side to allow his Morghasts past. Nagash unleashed every spell he could on the Eidolon, battering it with magic before his bodyguards hacked it to pieces, the aelven spirit-being suddenly disappearing in a watery blast. This little victory achieved, Nagash ordered his Spirit Hosts to ford the river and attack the aelven priest that was stealing his souls, but the Spirits shied away from the Isharann and cowered near the soul siphon. Prince Vhordrai, however, was not so cowardly and charged into the Morrsarr Guard that had tried to wipe out the Grave Guard. The eel riders did not survive the encounter.

SEIZING THE INITIATIVE

Martyn: Sam played an interesting tactic this battle round – he won the roll-off and let me go first. He knew I had very few units that could shoot, so I wouldn't do much damage in that phase. All of his units would also be striking first in combat in this battle round due to the Tides of Death rule, so he had that phase nailed down, too. What really hurt me was the hero phase. Because I was going first, I could resurrect a load of my Skeletons, which was handy, but it meant that Nagash was still just out of range with many of his spells. It was a devious move!

Seeing the Eidolon dissipate was a bitter blow to Volturnos – it would take a long time to recover that lost soul energy. Leaving the Namarti Thralls to hold the line against the looming Morghasts, he spurred Uasall onward, over the heads of the Morghasts and into the Bloodseeker Palanquin on the hill. He knew he could not fight Nagash, but he might be able to distract him long enough for Maughan to complete the ritual. Bellowing back orders, he sent the Ishlaen Guard across the river of souls to intercept the Spirit Hosts lurking there and to bolster the army's flank against the rampaging Vampire on his Zombie Dragon. Already he could hear the keening cries of the Terror of Maithnar as Prince Vhordrai hacked and slashed at it in a blood-mad rage. Perhaps the Allopexes would be able to hold the lunatic off, thought Volturnos as he charged at the Vampire Countess lounging on her throne, the Astra Solas held out before him in a challenge.

SOULS STOLEN
BATTLE ROUND THREE

5

TIDES OF DEATH
High Tide: In this battle round, units with the Tides of Death battle trait fight before any other units in the combat phase.

THE DEATH TOLL RISES

Martyn: The Eidolon of Mathlann was causing me all kinds of grief on the northern flank. It has an aura that enables nearby Idoneth to re-roll 1s to wound, it heals itself whenever it makes a charge and it can cause a vast amount of damage. So I hit it with every spell I could. Nagash was still out of range with some of his spells, but he managed to wound the Eidolon enough for the Morghasts to charge in and kill it in combat.

Nagash **(1)** unleashes his magical might on the Eidolon of Mathlann, casting Arcane Bolt, Soul Stealer (twice) and Decrepify on it, plus Spectral Grasp on the Graveyards to slow down the Idoneth nearby. The Bloodseeker Palanquin **(2)** casts Blood Siphon on the Eidolon, reducing it to just five wounds.

Nagash, the Wight King, Prince Vhordrai **(3)** and the Vampire Lord **(4)** all use Deathly Invocation to resurrect Skeleton Warriors **(5)** and Grave Guard. The Grave Guard fall back past the Morrsarr Guard but are then charged by the Akhelian Allopexes **(6)** and wiped out.

Prince Vhordrai's Zombie Dragon uses its Breath of Shyish on the Morrsarr Guard, killing one of them before Vhordrai kills the other two in combat.

A trio of Spirit Hosts **(7)** make for the river of souls and try to charge the Leviadon to gain ground but fail to reach it. They are then set upon by the Ishlaen Guard **(8)** as they race across the river to stop the Spirits attacking the Isharann **(9)** in the following turn.

The Morghasts **(10)** push past the Skeleton Warriors and charge the Eidolon. The aelven spirit construct almost kills a Morghast but is destroyed in return. The Morghasts are then charged by the Namarti Thralls **(11)**, who fell two of them with sweeping blows of their lanmari blades. Six Thralls die but three are brought back to life by Yranae **(12)**.

Volturnos flies over the undead army once more to attack the Bloodseeker Palanquin **(13)**, causing seven wounds on it.

The Terror of Maithnar **(14)** charges into Prince Vhordrai, causing five wounds, but taking eight in return from the blood-crazed Vampire.

SOULS STOLEN
BATTLE ROUND FOUR
💀 13

BATTLE ROUND FOUR: WHEN SOULS ARE UNBOUND

Maughan's eyes burned with arcane energy as captured souls spilled out from the stone monolith and congregated around Yranae's lurelight. They were rescuing the trapped souls, but the Great Necromancer was almost upon them. Volturnos had left the Isharann to their mission, intent on holding back the undead hordes whatever the cost – Maughan could just see him at the top of the hill slashing at a Vampire on a palanquin held aloft by a swirling mass of spirits. The Leviadon known as the Voidbeast surged past overhead heading straight for Nagash, while the nearby Namarti finally succeeded in destroying Nagash's Morghast bodyguards. Maughan looked across the river and sighed with relief as the First Sons of Príom and the Ethersea Marauders tore apart the Vampires and destroyed the force that was trying to flank the Idoneth. Then the top of the hill exploded in a supernova of dark magic.

LOCUS OF SHYISH
Martyn: There's a new ability in Legions of Nagash that is well worth knowing – Locus of Shyish. Every time a death wizard casts a spell from the Lore of the Vampires or Lore of the Deathmages on a 9+ (before any modifiers), they get to cast it again. It just so happens that when Nagash got in range to use his spells, I rolled 9+ a lot! At one point, Nagash cast Vile Transference on a 15 (because he has +3 to cast thanks to his staff Alakanash) and then caused three mortal wounds with it twice. The Locus ability is one you don't want to forget!

Every move Nagash made, the aelves anticipated it. No longer! The Great Necromancer thrust his blade Zefet-nebtar through the Leviadon, split open its shell, then wrenched what remained of its life essence from it. Turning, he saw Volturnos slay Countess Jaedla with a swift slice of his cutlass. Before the aelven lord could retreat out of harm's way, Nagash returned the favour, smashing Volturnos from his mount. He lay in the mud and did not move again. Nagash did not spare him another glance and commanded his Skeleton Warriors to advance down the hill once more. The Namarti Thralls that stood before them were quickly overwhelmed – the aelven priest was nearly within his grasp! Nagash cast his mystical eye over the battlefield and saw that his flank assault was in tatters, Prince Vhordrai lying in the dust as voracious sea creatures tore at the remains of his rotten mount. Nagash seethed with rage at the ineffectiveness of his servants.

TIDES OF DEATH
Ebb Tide: In this battle round, all units with the Tides of Death battle trait that retreat can still either shoot or charge in the same turn.

LET THE BLOOD FLOW

Sam: It was a tough choice deciding what unit to fight with first in my turn, but in the end I settled on the Allopexes. They had devoured two units so far this game and I intended to make Prince Vhordrai the third before he killed the Leviadon. The riders did only a single wound, but the Allopexes killed Vhordrai with their ferocious bites before they even got to use their scythed fins. They really are combat monsters!

INSOLENCE IS REWARDED WITH PAIN

Martyn: Sam chose the Allopexes to fight first, so I picked Nagash to attack the Leviadon. Nagash can dish out 30 damage in a single round of combat, so I was a little disappointed when he only did 10 to the Leviadon. Still, he more than half killed the beast in a single swipe and took only a single wound in return.

The Soulscryer (1) rescues another eight souls from the soul siphon, taking the total to 13. He also casts the Ritual of the tempest once more to stop Nagash and his undead minions from flying.

The Tidecaster (2) casts Arcane Bolt on the Morghasts and gravely wounds one of them.

Volturnos retreats to behind the Bloodseeker Palanquin before charging again. He topples the palanquin and kills the Vampire in combat.

The Allopexes (3) charge Prince Vhordrai and tear him and his Zombie Dragon to pieces.

The Voidbeast flies over the Morghasts to attack the Bloodseeker Palanquin but gets within 3" of Nagash (see Insolence is Rewarded with Pain, left) and is attacked by the Great Necromancer.

The Namarti Reavers use their storm fire to bring down the last two Morghasts. The Namarti Thralls, now unengaged, charge the Skeleton Warriors (4) and kill only three. The 'dead' Skeletons get back up and overwhelm the Thralls, wiping them out in combat.

Nagash attempts to cast Hand of Dust on the Leviadon but fails to cast the spell due to the Dritchleech swimming around the Soulrender (5). The Soulscryer also deploys a Cloud of Midnight so he cannot be the target of Nagash's spells. Foiled, Nagash casts Vile Transference (twice) on the Leviadon and kills it, but his other spells are negated by the Tidecaster or fail to cause any damage. Nagash then charges Volturnos and kills him with Zefet-nebtar.

The Spirit Hosts (6) claw at the Allopexes (7) and cause three mortal wounds, but lose two of their number to the sea monsters. Nearby, the Vampire Lord is slain by the Ishlaen Guard (8).

BATTLE ROUNDS FIVE AND SIX: THE LAST STAND

Harsh ripples in the ethersea told the Ishlaen Guard that their commander had fallen in battle. Turning their Fangmora Mounts around, they raced back towards the Isharann huddled around the foot of the soul siphon. Their ritual was almost complete, but the northern flank of the Idoneth forces had crumbled entirely and a mass of Skeletons was shambling down through the mausoleums and half-buried graves to find the Soulscryer.

As the Ishlaen Guard raced over the river of souls to place themselves between Nagash's legions and the Isharann, a wave of dark magic swept through the graveyards. The First Sons of Príom reined in their blinkered mounts as a regiment of mouldering Grave Guard rose from the burial grounds nearby, almost entirely surrounding the Idoneth forces. Looking up the hill, the Ishlaen Guard saw Nagash descend upon them – magic

FEROCIOUS SPEED

Sam: Honestly, I have never known a unit as fast as the Ishlaen Guard. They have a movement value of 14" as standard, but benefitted several times from the Give Them No Respite command ability (+3" move) and the Tides of Death, which enabled them to run and charge in the third battle round. In my last turn of the game they raced a full 20" across the battlefield to protect my Isharann heroes from being attacked by Martyn's Skeleton hordes. I'm glad I did that, too, because otherwise they might all have been killed!

leapt from his skeletal fingers and one of the Akhelians fell. Shevari the Tidecaster cried out as a lance of dark magic speared her – she refused to fall but was then blasted from her feet as Nagash's eyes blazed with necromantic energy.

And then the skeletal legions were upon them. The Grave Guard hacked at the Ishlaen Guard, dragging one from the saddle, but failing to push past the survivors. The Skeleton Warriors assaulted Lotann, but could not get their attacks past the ochtar familiar that floated near his shoulder, blades and cudgels at the ready to defend its master. As skeletal hands clawed at his robes, Maughan incanted the last words of his ritual and a flurry of souls burst forth from the soul siphon. The monolith shook as if alive, stone shattering as rocks tumbled from its apex. The brazier guttered and went out. His mission complete, Maughan called a hasty retreat.

SOULS STOLEN
BATTLE ROUND FIVE
19

TIDES OF DEATH
Low Tide: In this battle round, all units with the Tides of Death battle trait are treated as being in cover.

THE IDONETH DEEPKIN VICTORIOUS (BUT ONLY JUST)

Sam: Well, that was a bit too close for comfort. Had you won that roll-off for the battle round, I reckon you might well have won the game.

Martyn: It was close and there were quite a few points where the battle could have gone either way. You used the Tides of Death really well to coordinate your attacks – I think they're really going to shake up how people play Warhammer Age of Sigmar.

Sam: Agreed, though I think I had a bit of luck, too – I managed to get my Ritual of the Tempest to cast every turn and it stopped your powerful units from getting into combat early on.

Martyn: I planned to leap Nagash, the Morghasts and Vhordrai over my other units and into combat – that ritual really put a stop to that. I must admit, I also expected the Idoneth to be your typical fragile aelves, but the Akhelian Guard and the Allopexes were so hard to kill, not to mention ridiculously fast.

Sam: They were so dangerous – I was really impressed with both units. I would like to use bigger units of Namarti in the future, though – I really wanted to use the Soulrender's ability to bring them back and I only got to once! **DH**

Nagash gazed down at the aelven bodies piled up around his feet and stabbed at one with his blade. Zefet-nebtar howled with malevolent energy as it stripped the last sparks of life from the wounded aelf, who twitched once then lay still amidst the carnage. These were unlike any aelves Nagash had ever encountered – they reeked of Teclis's magic, yet there was something lurking beneath, something that intrigued the Great Necromancer greatly.

He inspected the aelves more closely and saw that many of them had no eyes. Interesting. The blind aelves also wore collars around their necks, deep scars running across their shoulders and chests. Nagash willed one of the corpses to rise into the air before him – salt water and blood dripped from its body and mingled with the mud below. Even in death the body gave off a magical aura, one that Nagash had come to associate with all aelven-kind. It was repulsive. He cast his mind easily into the corpse and searched for its soul, a morsel to devour in the wake of the battle. There was nothing there. Nagash discarded the body and hauled up another. No soul there either. He had sensed the soul energy of the aelves as they fought, had seen it blazing before him, yet now there was nothing. Curious. The Great Necromancer floated back up into the air, wailing spirits coalescing around him as they pleaded for merciful release. Nagash enjoyed their pitiful cries. He looked over the ruins of the soul siphon where it lay damming the river, departed souls flowing over and around the rocks. It would take time to rebuild, but that did not concern Nagash. Time meant nothing to the dead.

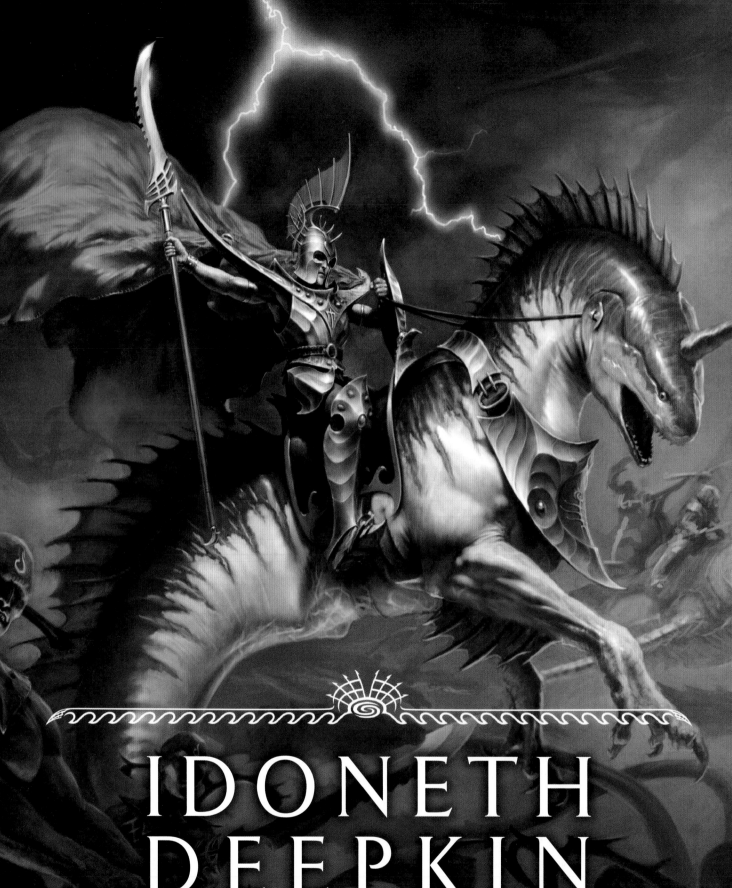

IDONETH DEEPKIN

The Idoneth Deepkin are a mysterious race of aelves who dwell in secrecy upon the deepest seabeds of the Mortal Realms. When they emerge from the seclusion that they strive so keenly to protect, they bring with them a ghostly manifestation of their strange aquatic environment, and the ferocious beasts of the abyss. In their wake they leave ruin, and the unsettlingly serene forms of sleepers who will never awaken – those whose very souls have been plundered...

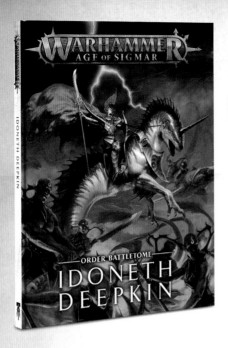

THE PERFECT COMPOSITION

Hall of Fame is a celebration of the finest miniatures in the world and the myriad factors that make them so iconic. This month, miniatures designer Darren Latham tells us what he thinks makes a great Citadel miniature and picks his nomination for the Hall of Fame.

DARREN LATHAM

Darren has been part of the Citadel miniatures design team for the last five years and before that he was a member of the 'Eavy Metal team for seven years. This is the second time that Darren has nominated a model for the Citadel Hall of Fame. Last time it was Deathmaster Snikch – what model will he pick this time?

As regular readers will be aware, Hall of Fame underwent a revamp a couple of issues ago, enabling us to take a closer look at what truly makes a great Citadel miniature. So far in this new format, miniatures design manager Ben Jefferson has talked about the importance of narrative in a model, while miniatures designer Matt Holland enlightened us on poses. But what does miniatures designer Darren Latham consider the key ingredient in a great Citadel miniature?

Darren: Coming from a painting background, a model that's fun to paint is a key consideration for me. But what I consider to be a crucial factor in any great Citadel miniature is composition.

WHAT IS COMPOSITION?

A model is composed of lots of elements, all of which need to work together in harmony to create a great miniature. The composition of a model takes into account its pose, the story behind it, the overall flow of the model, the shapes within its design, the textures that are used on it and where they are placed, the distribution of details across the model, its focal points… the list is very long! The ultimate goal with any miniature is that you should, at a glance, be able to read it – to see what's going on. You may have heard the phrase 'golden angle' before – we use it in photography a lot – it's the angle at which all the key elements of the model are visible, such as weapons, faces, magical items and so on. Vandus Hammerhand is a great example of this – you can see everything that's happening on the model immediately. Nothing obscures anything important, which is a key consideration in miniatures design.

SHAPE AND BALANCE

From the golden angle you should be able to see the shape of a model. Many action-pose models have an 'X' shape – the Phoenix Lords Baharroth and Jain Zar both do – while others like Vandus and Belisarius Cawl are triangular. You can also see how well the key elements are balanced across a model from the golden angle. Baharroth, for example, has his sword raised, which balances out the Hawk's Talon gun in his other hand – he doesn't look top-heavy or awkward. You'll also find that details are often balanced across a model, in Baharroth's case spirit stones. They're not all clumped together but positioned around the model to provide areas of interest while helping to explain the story behind it.

> **"A model is composed of lots of elements, all of which need to work together in harmony to create a great miniature."**

DIRECTIONALITY

Directionality is a key feature in the composition of a model – Matt touched on it last month when he talked about a model's pose. A model will normally have a single direction to its movement, which helps explain what the model is doing. Baharroth's directionality is diagonally upwards, suggesting he's about to take flight, while Jain Zar's is diagonally downwards, showing that she's leaping into a fight. In both cases the line along the model's arms draws you towards the head – the focal part of the model. Another example is the Curseling – his weapons and tabard are all vertical, giving him an implacable, solid appearance. This contrasts with the diagonal line that runs up from his feathered cape, through his torso and up to his mutated left arm that is whispering into his ear, drawing your attention to the focal parts of the model – in this case the Curseling's head and his staff. But what model truly epitomises composition for me? Turn the page to find out.

AN ORIGINAL PICK

Darren: The first time I nominated a model for the Citadel Hall of Fame was way back in 2010 and I picked Deathmaster Snikch (now the Skaven Assassin) sculpted by Seb Perbet. I mentioned how great the model's pose was, how his three blades formed the Clan Eshin symbol, how his cape frames him, how he looms over his next victim. It was all about the composition of the model, I just didn't realise it at the time!

"Vandus Hammerhand (1) is one of Seb Perbet's models," says Darren. "Vandus has a triangular shape to him, with the haft of his hammer forming a strong vertical line through the centre of the model. His pennant, helmet plume and his Dracoth's tail all share the same shape and direction, bringing unity to the flow of the model. The Dracoth's head has been angled to face the viewer, while the lightning bolts on Vandus' helmet direct your eye towards his head – his focal point. Seb used the same trick on the shell-shaped crown of the new Akhelian King model."

"Steve Buddle's Belisarius Cawl (2) is also triangular in shape, with his axe forming a strong vertical line to the top of the triangle. Cawl also has an S shape to his body, suggesting that it is inhuman and unnatural. His mechadendrites and the power cables on his wargear echo that shape and reinforce it. Note how – despite the fact that Belisarius Cawl is a really busy model – none of his weapons or pieces of wargear interfere with his torso and head, which can still be seen clearly from the golden angle."

"Both Baharroth (3) and Jain Zar (4) by Jes Goodwin are X-shaped models with strong diagonal lines running through them – Baharroth's sword and gun run parallel, for example, crossing over the other diagonal line that runs up from his right foot, though his body and along his left arm. Their poses and directionality suggest a lot of grace and a high level of energy. Note how Jain Zar's leather straps and tabard have been painted the same spot colour, showing a balance of details across the model."

"Seb's Curseling (5) has a classic H shape – he's pretty symmetrical despite his mutations, and his wide stance and vertical weapons suggests immovability. I love how you're drawn to the model's head by what is essentially another head whispering in its ear – it's a very clever way to signpost you towards the model's most important and focal feature."

"Despite the fact that Belisarius Cawl is a really busy model, none of his weapons or pieces of wargear interfere with his torso and head, which can still be seen clearly from the golden angle."

CITADEL
HALL OF FAME INDUCTEE

ARCHAON EVERCHOSEN
Designed by Seb Perbet | Nominated by Darren Latham

"There is a strong directionality to Archaon," says Darren. "His sword and shield are both angled in the same direction (1), giving him a plunging, aggressive look, like he is about to smash down into something. His head matches the angle of his wargear."

"Seb was really clever with the distribution of details – an important compositional element. Dorghar needed to be interesting but not overshadow Archaon. That's why many of his details – the skulls embedded in his flesh (2) and the eight-pointed star branded on his flank (3) – are on his back, not his front."

"Making a model with three heads (4 and 5) is no easy task. They also have to evoke the image of their particular god without being overwhelming, while fitting around each other in such a way that they don't obscure the details of the one next to them – it's a tough balancing act to pull off. Placing the central head above the other two suggests superiority over them, but also helps direct your eye to Archaon sitting behind them."

"The crows (6) may seem like a casual addition to the model, but they scale the piece. You know the size of a crow, so now you know how big Archaon is!"

Darren: For me, Archaon epitomises everything I've talked about when it comes to the composition of a Citadel miniature. Archaon is surely the pinnacle of Seb's craft as a miniatures designer – the sheer scale of the model is impressive enough, but the composition of the piece is a true work of art.

There are so many elements to this model, but all of them are balanced in perfect harmony. Take Dorghar – Archaon's daemonic steed. Dorghar is huge, yet his whole design – his shape in particular – is used to draw your eye towards Archaon. If your attention is caught by Dorghar's fiery tail, you quickly find your eyes moving up the model, following the S-shaped curve of Dorghar's body up towards Archaon. Dorghar's wings spread out on either side of Archon, framing him. Even the fingers between the wing membranes (there are eight on each side – the number of points on a Chaos star) all point towards him. It would have been very easy for Dorghar's heads to distract from Archaon, but they actually point upwards like an arrowhead towards him, with the blue Tzeentch head directly beneath him. Another little touch that I love is the wall that Dorghar is smashing apart with his tail – compositionally it balances out the wings at the top of the model, but this narrative element also helps explain the coiled strength and power of this massive beast.

Then there's Archaon himself. Considering the size of Dorghar, it's easy to forget that Archaon is also huge – easily over 10 feet tall. The skulls around his neck help scale him, giving you an understanding of his size. Seb has sculpted Archaon leaning forward, looming over his foes, with his helmet angled down. There's a lot of arrogance and deadly intent in Archaon's pose, emphasised by the diagonal line running through his weapons and eye-line. His helmet plume mirrors the shape of Dorghar's tail at the bottom of the model. DH

A LOOMING PRESENCE
In this silhouette you can see the diagonal lines that run through the Archaon model. His sword, eye-line, shield and Dorghar's arm are all parallel, giving the impression that Archaon is about to smash down into an unfortunate victim.

FIND YOUR LOCAL STORE

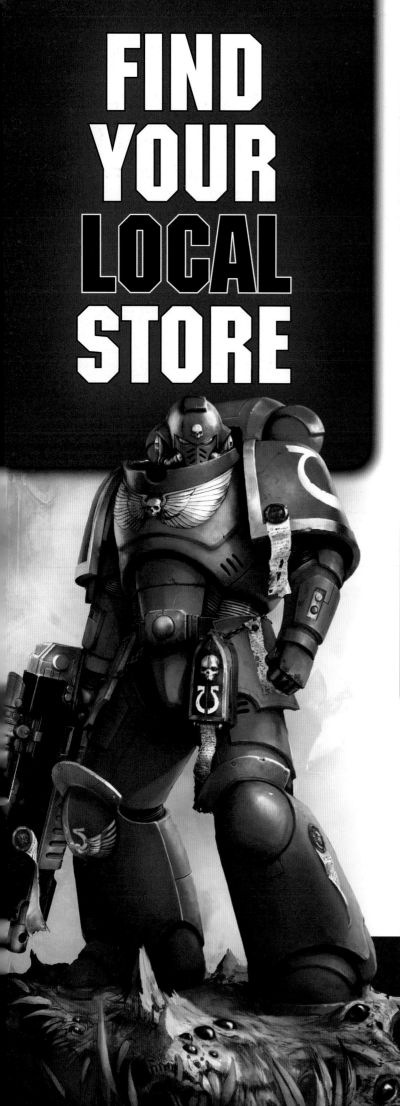

GAMES WORKSHOP AND WARHAMMER STORES

IMMERSE YOURSELVES IN OUR WORLDS AND TALK ABOUT YOUR HOBBY. OUR FRIENDLY STAFF WILL TEACH YOU HOW TO COLLECT, BUILD, PAINT AND PLAY WITH YOUR MINIATURES!

INDEPENDENT STOCKISTS

WITH OVER 2,000 INDEPENDENT STOCKISTS AROUND THE GLOBE, SELLING A RANGE OF OUR BEST SELLING PRODUCTS, YOUR LOCAL STORE IS NEVER TOO FAR AWAY.

FIND YOUR NEAREST STORE:
GAMES-WORKSHOP.COM/STORE-FINDER

REMEMBER, WE'RE ALWAYS OPEN AT:
GAMES-WORKSHOP.COM

A TALE OF FOUR WARLORDS

Across the Mortal Realms, malign portents herald a time of great turmoil. Warriors gather and armies muster as those who would write their own legends sense that this is the time foretold for them to set out upon their own path to glory. This is A Tale of Four Warlords...

T he four warlords return to the pages of White Dwarf once more, bringing with them new reinforcements to aid them in their eternal (well, for the next few months at the very least) crusade to dominate the Mortal Realms.

Their challenge this month was to paint enough units to make their armies battle ready for a 2,000-point matched play game – a task that three out of the four warlords achieved with commendable vigour. Yes, that's right, only three out of the four completed this month's challenge! "I got distracted," says Andy, sheepishly. You can see what distracted our paragon of Order above – it's pretty big! We did think about forgiving him for his transgression, but rules are there to be followed – Andy wasn't allowed any biscuits until he'd repented. As we write this article, he still hasn't been allowed any…

Interestingly, alongside painting new units for their armies, all four warlords elected to add at least one monster to their collection. Jes painted another Great Unclean One for his army of Nurgle Daemons, while Anthony picked a Mourngul for his Death army. Nick rekindled his love of giants (it must be something to do with his height) and painted a Gargant for his Beastclaw Raiders, while Andy… well, as we said before, you can see what he added to his Daughters of Khaine above.

Our challenge for our four warlords next month is to paint a wizard for their army. A surprisingly easy challenge, we think you'll agree. Just what are we up to? Well, you'll just have to wait until next month to find out. In the meantime, if you're also taking part in our warlords challenge, make sure you show us some pictures of your models on the White Dwarf Facebook page – we'd love to see what you've been painting.

A TALE OF FOUR WARLORDS
First appearing in 1997, A Tale of Four Warlords is one of the most iconic series to ever feature in White Dwarf. In it, four eager hobbyists are given six months to build up a mighty army, with challenges to meet each month along the way. Many hobbyists like to use the Tale of Four Warlords format to inspire their own collecting efforts, by following along, collecting their own force with the same monthly challenges, or by getting together with others to set their own stage goals. If you're doing this, be sure to write in and let us know!

BEASTCLAW RAIDERS

Nick Bayton has been using the festive period to channel his inner Ogor by consuming vast quantities of food in the hope of communing with the mighty Gorkamorka. He's been painting some models, too.

NICK BAYTON

Nick, or 'Hobby Bates', is a veteran of painting challenges. Seriously, this guy has hit more painting deadlines than you've had hot dinners. Probably twice as many. In fact, in the time it took you to read this bio, Nick painted three models.

Nick's three packs of Mournfang Cavalry in all their barbaric, bestial glory. Each unit bears a unique banner to help set it apart on the battlefield.

Nick began this month's additions by painting four more Mournfang Cavalry, though his choice of assembly options seemed a little odd at first…

"The four models I built this month comprised three Mournfang banner bearers and a Skalg leader. I had previously painted two units of four Mournfang Cavalry, each led by a Skalg, but as I had yet to decide upon the icon and unifying colour I would use for the army, I left the banners out until now. Building that specific combination enabled me to divide my Mournfang Cavalry into three new units of four models, each with its own Skalg and banner bearer.

"I eventually chose a fairly bright unifying colour for the army, to contrast nicely with the earthy, muted tones that dominate each model, whilst complementing their overall icy feel. I achieved this with a basecoat of Thousand Sons Blue, a wash of Druchii Violet, then a layer of Thousand Sons Blue followed by Ahriman Blue. Over the next couple of months, I will be adding the same colours to various tabards and patches of cloth on existing models in the army to serve as a spot colour. On that note, the army icon I eventually settled on was one featured in the Beastclaw Raiders battletome, and was achieved using the techniques described within. I'll also be adding that symbol to models throughout the army on banners, as tattoos or on bare patches of cloth – wherever is appropriate."

Whilst browsing various painting guides on the Warhammer TV YouTube channel, Nick came across a handy guide on painting ice weaponry. This inspired not only his Yhetees last month, but also his latest additions. "By carefully filing down the Chaos star etched into the large rock carried by the Gargant, I was able to paint it up as a giant (forgive the pun) shard of ice. I used the same effect on the throwing spears strapped to the back of the Icebrow Hunter. I find that making use of identifying features such as this can really add to the visual impact of an army."

Despite adding only a handful of models to his collection this month, Nick's army now comfortably exceeds the 2000-point pitched battle goal.

1

2

Nick's goal when assembling his Icebrow Hunter was to ensure that it represented all of the weapon options available to it on its warscroll. To do so, he scavenged a spare crossbow from the Stonehorn/Thundertusk kit and swapped it for the club normally held in the model's right hand **(1)**. To finish kitting him out, Nick fitted a club from the Ogors box to the model's left hand before adding a gut plate from the same kit, then mounted the brace of throwing spears to the Hunter's back.

Nick carefully painted his army's symbol **(2)** on many of his models.

DAUGHTERS OF KHAINE

Our representative for the forces of Order Andy Keddie has flouted the rules this month and painted a huge centrepiece for his army instead of more troops. It is Morathi, though, so can you blame him?

ANDY KEDDIE

As we write this issue, Andy is taking a long-deserved rest following the Warhammer World New Year's Open Day. Okay, that's not strictly true – he's trying to get some more Sisters of Slaughter painted. Keep going, Andy!

A whole load of snakes – that's what Andy's painted this month. Having painted Morathi, he's now inspired to paint his infantry for next month.

This month, it's fair to say that Andy has gone snake crazy! Not only has he painted Morathi for his army, he has also painted three Bloodwrack Medusae – but, as we pointed out earlier, no more Witch Aelves to make his army ready for 2,000-point matched play games. We quizzed him about this. Thumb screws were involved.

"I got my hands on Morathi and all my plans to paint more infantry units went out the window," says Andy. "Both versions of Morathi are incredible miniatures – the details on them are sublime – and I just had to paint them. I've got a Cauldron of Blood in my army, but we all know that Morathi is the real centrepiece for the Daughters of Khaine – there was no way I was going to collect an army without her in it. My army actually comes to around 2,500 points now, which is fine for casual games, but, yes, I know, I need to paint more battleline units. Another 10 Sisters of Slaughter are on my painting desk – I'll get them done for next month, I promise."

But Morathi wasn't the only model(s) Andy painted this month. "I managed to get my hands on three more Bloodwrack Medusae, says Andy with a cheeky grin. "Honestly, these are the models that made me want to collect Daughters of Khaine in the first place (that was before I saw Morathi, of course). They are excellent models with loads of character and I think several of them, along with a few Blood Sisters and Blood Seekers, will look great slithering around on the battlefield. I love how the Witch Aelves are like the public face of the Daughters of Khaine, but behind the scenes they really are truly monstrous to behold – the Medusae really capture that horror in my opinion." Andy decided to paint each of his Medusae a different colour, inspired by the painting guides for the Gorgons in Battletome: Daughters of Khaine. "I did this for a few reasons," says Andy. "First, it helps to identify them on the battlefield. Second, it means I can give them each a name and personality and link it to the model. Last, they're magical snake-aelf-ladies – they don't have to be the same colour!"

MAGGOTKIN OF NURGLE

Pus, slime, mould and rot. No, we're not talking about Jes Bickham's breakfast (he's a crumpet man), but rather what he's been painting this month; the nastiest Great Unclean One of them all – Rotigus!

Jes Bickham – creative writing manager, former Dwarfer, aspiring wizard and lover of Nurgling Green paint. What is there to say about Jes that you don't already know? Well, he really likes the Sloppity Bilepiper and that's a fact you didn't know!

"It's a bold statement, but the Sloppity Bilepiper might well be one of my favourite Citadel miniatures of all time," says Jes. "It's certainly in my top five. A lot of people think he's jolly and happy, prancing around, but I think he's terrifying, convulsing around in the grips of a feverish disease that will eventually kill him. The model (and the story behind it) is so grim and wonderfully characterful. I decided to paint his gutpipes with a human skin tone to suggest he'd been busy skinning someone to make his infernal instrument. His hood is a regal purple and the one on his marotter red – two of the spot colours I've used on the heroes in my army to help them stand out from the hordes of Plaguebearers, Beasts and Nurglings."

Jes also painted Rotigus Rainfather, the second Great Unclean One to join the ranks of his army. "I'm aiming to complete a warscroll battalion from Battletome: Maggotkin of Nurgle – the Thricefold Befoulment," says Jes. "It contains three Great Unclean Ones, which is convenient because you can make three different-looking models from the kit. I already have one Great Unclean One and now Rotigus – I reckon I'll be painting a third for next month's wizard challenge!

"Like the Bilepiper, I gave Rotigus a purple cowl to show his noble status. I used Naggaroth Night as a basecoat followed by layers of Xereus Purple, Genestealer Purple and Slaanesh Grey – it's one of the few parts on my models where I layered the paint – the rest of my army has been washed and drybrushed. I also painted a third Beast of Nurgle this month to give me a trio of the horrible little blighters. I'm also part way through painting a Feculent Gnarlmaw – a model I've wanted to paint for months but only just got around to. I will have my Garden of Nurgle!"

JES BICKHAM
Jes originally planned to build an army of Nurgle that included mortals, but the Daemons of Nurgle released earlier this year grabbed his attention so much he decided to stick with them for the moment. The mortals are sad about this.

Rotigus presides over Jes's strange council of Nurgle. The Sloppity Bilepiper plays a jig on his gutpipes while the Beast of Nurgle wiggles along to the tune.

LEGIONS OF NAGASH

Anthony has been living up to his epithet of the Warlord of Death, swelling the ranks of his unholy legion with a fearsome combination of overwhelming numbers and voracious bloodlust.

ANTHONY SALIBA

Over the course of this series, Anthony has proven himself to be an unstoppable painting machine, even putting notorious hobby hero Nick Bayton to shame with the overwhelming quantity of miniatures in his deathly legion.

Anthony has further reinforced the vampiric theme of his army by adding a flight of five Vargheists, with a sixth member of the unit already underway.

Anthony excitedly recounted his painting exploits this month, barely able to conceal the manic glint in his eye. If his plans for this army are to be believed, it appears that he won't be satisfied until he has an Undead legion to rival that of the Great Necromancer himself! Bold claims such as units of 300 Zombies, Skeletons and Grave Guard were bandied about like the insane ramblings of a doomsayer. "Don't worry – I've not gone mad (*yet!* – E*d*). I'll get them painted eventually. I also plan on adding Nagash to my army once I've finished all of his Mortarchs, so I think he'll forgive me… won't he?"

We're not convinced. Nagash is not known for his leniency and suffers no rivals. We think Anthony'd better tread (or paint) carefully, just to be safe.

Anthony's newest additions consist of a large, shambling horde of 30 Zombies and five bestial Vargheists (he didn't finish the sixth in time, but we'll let him off!), taking his army just over the 2000-point goal. However, never one to rest on his laurels, Anthony bolstered his deathly host further still by adding a monstrous Mourngul to terrorize his opponents on the battlefield.

"I couldn't resist adding one of these fiendish creatures to my collection. After painting so many patches of rotten flesh (*on account of painting no less than 50 Zombies over the past few months!* – E*d*), it made a refreshing change to tackle large areas of skin. I used a lighter pallet of colours to emphasise the Mourngul's otherworldly nature – it's at once a spectral and physical entity after all, and I'm very satisfied with the result.

"I've been feverishly leafing through the Legions of Nagash book in preparation for my rematch against Nick. There are a number of different allegiance abilities to choose from, but I think I'll use the Soulblight rules for the moment, as Tamar Von Drak currently leads my army from atop her Coven Throne. I may switch things up later on as I add other Mortarchs to the army." **DH/SG**

The Mourngul serves as a towering centrepiece in Anthony's ever-growing legion of the dead. His choice of pallid skin contrasts nicely with the rotten flesh tones of the Zombies accompanying it.

NEXT MONTH

The winds of magic are blowing strong in the Mortal Realms right now, so we have asked our four warlords to paint a wizard, sorcerer or otherworldly magic user to add to their army. But we've also set them another challenge – something they will be very excited about...

DUELS OF THE
CRYSTAL LABYRINTH

Deep in the Realm of Chaos lies the Crystal Labyrinth, the domain of Tzeentch. Down its ever-changing and kaleidoscopic corridors wander powerful sorcerers who compete against rivals to further their ambitions and machinations. Will you join them?

Welcome to Duels of the Crystal Labyrinth, a minigame where you and your friends take on the role of battling Tzeentch Sorcerers competing against one another in deadly magical duels. In this game you'll be able to cast devastating magic, conjure daemons to send into the fray and put together complex combinations of different types of spells that would make Tzeentch himself tremble! What's even better is you'll find all the rules needed to play over the next few pages and you'll find the board for the game on the back cover (which you're free to photocopy, if you wish) so you can get stuck into the action straight away!

WHAT DO YOU NEED TO PLAY?

To get started, the players will each need a copy of the gameboard, which you can find the gameboard on the back of the magazine. Each player will also need about 15 to 20 six-sided dice. You'll often see the rules refer to these dice as a D6. If a rule refers to a D3 instead, roll a six-sided dice and half the result, rounding up.

Each player will need a Citadel miniature to represent their sorcerer. This can be any suitable miniature but we recommend something like the Gaunt Summoner, a Magister or perhaps even an Ogroid Thaumaturge.

Lastly the players will need some Pink, Blue and Brimstone Horrors for the lesser daemons. There's potential for 18 of any one type to be in play at once – this is somewhat likely with Brimstone Horrors, unlikely with Blue Horrors and very unlikely with Pink Horrors, though, so you shouldn't need too many. One set of Pink Horrors and two sets of Blue and Brimstones will be ample. If you or a friend has a Daemons of Tzeentch army you will likely have more than enough for both players to use already.

THE GAMEBOARD

Place the gameboards together as shown below. The resulting board is split into two halves, one for each player. Each features a large circle displaying the mark of Tzeentch. Place your sorcerer here. Each half of the gameboard also features three tiles with three large circles to place your lesser daemons in when summoned. Each of these tiles also features three smaller squares to indicate wounds on your lesser daemons and a square to indicate any Traps.

VICTORY

The goal of the game is simple – you must defeat the enemy sorcerer and continue on your quest deeper into the Crystal Labyrinth. Each sorcerer starts with 18 wounds and is defeated when they are reduced to zero.

SET UP

Each player sets up their sorcerer on the large circle with the mark of Tzeentch in their section of the gameboard and then places three dice in the Wounds slots each showing the value of 6. The duel can now commence!

Both players roll a dice and the winner chooses if they wish to go first or second. There is a handicap for going first, which means going both first and second has its own advantages.

THE PLAYER TURN

After the roll-off to decide who goes first, the players take it in turns until one sorcerer is defeated and the other is crowned victorious. Each player turn has three distinct phases:

1. The dice in the player's Destiny Pool are generated.
2. The player makes their Spell Actions.
3. The player makes their Attack Actions. ▶

Below: The gameboard set up, ready for the start of the game. Each player's sorcerer is stood in the circular space marked with the Mark of Tzeentch and each player has rolled their Destiny dice and placed them in their Destiny Pool. The Gaunt Summoner will be taking the first turn so has rolled only four dice.

THE DESTINY POOL

On each section of the gameboard you will find nine square slots called the Destiny Pool. This is the player's magical reserve from which their sorcerer will draw power to cast spells. In all game turns except the first, the player has nine dice in their Destiny Pool. At the start of a player's turn roll nine dice and place them in the Destiny Pool. You may find it useful to group these by value as the numbers relate to the different lores of magic you have at your disposal.

During the game the player can keep any of the dice in their Destiny Pool into their opponent's turn to use to dispel magic. If at the start of their own turn, a player has dice remaining in their Destiny Pool they can choose to keep these dice (if so, only generate new dice up to the total of nine), or discard these dice and generate a new Destiny Pool of nine dice.

FIRST TURN HANDICAP

Striking first in a duel gives your sorcerer the element of surprise. They can cast spells before the enemy has had chance to raise their protective wards and other defences. However, lashing out first requires the sorcerer to sacrifice some of their power in place of speed. To represent this, the player that goes first in the duel only generates four dice for their Destiny Pool in their first turn. In subsequent turns they generate back up to a total of nine as usual.

SPELL ACTIONS

As a sorcerer of Tzeentch you have lots of powerful spells at your disposal. You will be able to conjure all kinds of lesser daemons to do your bidding, you'll be able to bathe the enemy in fire, trap them behind magical prisons of crackling blue energy and whisper subtle suggestions in their ears. With 18 spells there are endless combinations and strategies to employ.

There are six lores of magic to choose from and these correspond to the values on each of the dice in your Destiny Pool.

For example, the Third Lore of Magic is that of Duplicity. Any of the dice in a player's Destiny Pool with the value of 3 can be used to cast spells from that lore. How many dice the player has with the same value in their Destiny Pool dictates how powerful the spell can be. So, for example, a 1st level Duplicity spell requires one dice with a value of 3, a 2nd level Duplicity spell requires two dice with a value of 3, and so on.

To make a Spell Action, the player chooses a spell they have sufficient dice for and declares the target. The spell description will list what can be targeted; usually the player will be able to target either the enemy sorcerer or one of the tiles on the gameboard that has lesser daemons in it. To cast the chosen spell, discard the dice from the Destiny Pool and apply the spell effect.

In their own turn, a player can make as many Spell Actions as they have dice available for in their Destiny Pool. You may wish to save some dice, however, as these can be used to dispel your opponent's spells in their turn.

DISPELLING

If a player has dice remaining in their Destiny Pool they can attempt to dispel any of their opponent's Spell Actions. If a player wishes to dispel a Spell Action they must declare they are doing so once the spell and target have been chosen but before the effects are applied.

The player attempting the dispel takes as many dice as they choose from those remaining in their Destiny Pool that all have the same value. The value of the dice does not need to match that of the spell being cast. The player rolls these dice to create a **dispel score**. The player making the Spell Action rolls the dice required for the spell to create a **casting score**. If the dispel score equals or beats the casting score then the spell has been dispelled. Discard the dice used from each player's Destiny Pool but apply no effect from the spell. ▶

EXAMPLE 1: DISPELLING

The Gaunt Summoner attempts to cast Infernal Flames, a Third level spell from the Lore of Conflagration. He has four dice with a value of 5, and so uses three of these to cast the spell. The Magister decides he will attempt to dispel. In the Magister's Destiny Pool he has four dice with the values 1, 3, 3 and 5, so takes the two dice with a value of 3 and rolls them to create the dispel score, scoring 9! The Gaunt Summoner rolls the three dice used for Infernal Flames and also scores 9. As the dispel score and casting score are equal, the spell is dispelled and no effects are applied. Both players discard the dice they rolled.

TYPES OF SPELL

Across the six lores of magic are five different types of spell: **CRYSTALLINE WARDS**, **MACHINATION SPELLS**, **DUPLICITY SPELLS**, **DAMAGE SPELLS**, and **CONJURATION SPELLS**. Some of these spell types have special rules, which are described below.

CRYSTALLINE WARDS

The First lore of magic (The Lore Crystalline) allows your sorcerer to cast a special kind of spell known as a **CRYSTALLINE WARD**. This is a magical shield that can protect your sorcerer from attacks both magical and physical.

The target for a **CRYSTALLINE WARD** must be your sorcerer. If successfully cast, place a dice in the Ward slot to indicate the level of the ward (1, 2 or 3). Once cast, this spell stays in play until the ward is shattered. Each player can only have one **CRYSTALLINE WARD** in play at any time but can replace it with a more powerful one. **CRYSTALLINE WARDS** protect against **DAMAGE SPELLS** from the and Attack Actions from enemy lesser daemons.

If the sorcerer is targeted by a **DAMAGE SPELL** compare the level of the spell with that of the ward. If the spell level is less than the ward level the spell has no effect and the ward remains in play. If the spell level equals or beats that of the ward, the spell still has no effect but the ward is shattered and removed from play. If an Attack Action is made against a sorcerer with a ward, the ward is shattered regardless of its level but no wounds are inflicted.

MACHINATION SPELLS

The Lore of Machinations allows your sorcerer to cast magical prisons onto your opponent's tiles to trap their lesser daemons. There are three levels of **MACHINATION SPELL**, with each level indicating how many lesser daemons it can trap. To successfully cast a **MACHINATION SPELL** the level of the spell needs to be equal to or higher than the number of lesser daemons on the target tile. Once cast, place a dice or token in the status slot on the tile to indicate a trap is in play. Trapped lesser daemons cannot be targeted by Spell Actions or Attack Actions but also do not prevent you from making Attack Actions against the enemy sorcerer (see below).

The target tile is affected until the start of your next turn. Lesser daemons trapped by a **MACHINATION SPELL** cannot be used to make Attack Actions, cannot be targeted by Spell Actions and new lesser daemons cannot be placed on affected tiles by any means.

CONJURATION SPELLS

The Lore of Conjuration gives your sorcerer the power to summon lesser daemons into the duel, to protect them from attack and to launch vicious attacks of their own upon the enemy.

There are three types of lesser daemon: Pink Horrors, Blue Horror and Brimstone Horrors. When a player conjures lesser daemons they can place them onto available slots on any of their tiles. Each tile has space for three lesser

EXAMPLE 2: ATTACK ACTIONS

The Magister decides to declare an Attack Action with a tile holding three Pink Horrors. The Gaunt Summoner has two models on each of his tiles and so the Attack Action must be made against one of these tiles and cannot be made against the Gaunt Summoner himself. The Magister chooses the tile with two Blue Horrors and rolls an attack dice for each of his lesser daemons (the three Pink Horrors) scoring 6, 5 and 2. The Gaunt Summoner rolls an attack dice for each of his Blue Horrors in the tile (two) scoring 6 and 3. The two 6s are paired, resulting in no wounds, then the 5 and the 3 are paired, resulting in one wound being inflicted by Magister's Pink Horrors. The remaining dice has no dice to be paired with and so automatically inflicts a wound too. In total the attacking player, the Magister, inflicts two wounds.

EXAMPLE 3: WOUNDS
A tile with one Pink Horror is targeted by Greater Fireblast (1), which inflicts four wounds. Two wounds are allocated to the Pink Horror and it is slain, and the two remaining wounds are discarded as there are no more lesser daemons on the tile. Now the Spell Action has been resolved the Split rule comes into play and the player sets up two Blue Horrors on the tile (2).

daemons and this can be a mix of the different types. The larger lesser daemons (Pink and Blue Horrors) each have two wounds each. You can find the wounds value and any special rules a lesser daemon has on their card in the Liber Arcana. (over the page) There is a small square next to each lesser daemon slot which can be marked with a counter or dice to indicate when a lesser daemon is wounded.

ATTACK ACTIONS

Once you have made all your Spell Actions, the last phase in a player's turn is dedicated to Attack Actions. Each player's side of the gameboard has three tiles under their control. Each of these tiles can be used to make one Attack Action in the player's turn if it has lesser daemons on it. When making an Attack Action the player must first choose a target. The target of an Attack Action must be an enemy tile with lesser daemons on it or, if there are no tiles with lesser daemons on them or all lesser daemons are trapped by **Machination Spells**, the player can instead target the enemy sorcerer.

To resolve an Attack Action, both players take a dice for each of their lesser daemons on the tiles involved. These dice are not taken from your Destiny Pool. Roll all the dice and pair the highest dice from the attacking player with the highest dice from the defending player and so forth. The player with the higher score in each pair inflicts a wound upon the other's tile. Draws inflict no wounds and any unpaired dice automatically inflict a wound. To make an Attack Action against the enemy sorcerer, no dice are involved. Instead each model automatically inflicts a wound upon the sorcerer. A sorcerer can quickly perish if the opponent's lesser daemons are left unopposed!

INFLICTING WOUNDS

Attack Actions and some Spell Actions can inflict wounds on enemy models. Each sorcerer starts with 18 wounds, represented by three dice in the Wounds slots on their gameboard. Each time wounds are inflicted on a sorcerer reduce the total shown on the dice. When the sorcerer is reduced to zero wounds, the game ends immediately and the other player is the victor.

Conjured lesser daemons are much weaker. Brimstone Horrors have only a single wound and the larger Pink and Blue Horrors have two wounds each. When wounds are inflicted on a tile with lesser daemons on it the owning player decides how the wounds are allocated. When a model is reduced to zero wounds it is slain and removed from play. If all the lesser daemons in a tile have been slain any remaining wounds inflicted by the Attack or Spell action are ignored.

Pink and Blue Horrors have special rules that allow them to spilt into further Blue or Brimstone Horrors, as indicated on their card (found in the Liber Arcana, over the page). This rule takes effect after the Spell or Attack Action has been resolved and thus any remaining wounds inflicted have already been discarded before they are set up on the tile, so a Spell or Attack action that causes a Pink or Blue Horror to split can never harm the resulting Blue or Brimstone Horrors.

YOU'RE READY TO PLAY

These are all the rules you need to play the game. You'll find the Liber Arcana, featuring the six Lores of Magic, over the page and you'll find the gameboard on the back cover. So, grab a friend, some models to represent your sorcerer and their lesser daemons and see if you have what it takes to triumph in the Crystal Labyrinth! SP

HINTS & TIPS
When you start playing you'll quickly find there are lots of different tactics you can employ. While it's tempting to cast every spell possible out of your Destiny Pool, it can leave you open to a counter attack so it's always wise to try to keep some dice to use to dispel your opponent's spells.

If you're on the back foot, a good defensive strategy is to try and summon one lesser daemon onto each tile. Although the individual daemons will be weak in Attack Actions, it will require the opposing player to dedicate all their Attack Actions (or some Spell Actions) to clear them off, keeping your Sorcerer safe from harm.

LIBER ARCANA

LORE CRYSTALLINE

1ST LEVEL - MYSTIC SHIELD
CRYSTALLINE WARD Target your sorcerer. Protects against Attack Actions and 1st level spells marked **DAMAGE SPELL**. Place a dice in your 'Ward' slot with value 1 to show a ward is in play.

2ND LEVEL - ELDRITCH BARRIER
CRYSTALLINE WARD Target your sorcerer. Protects against Attack Actions and 1st and 2nd level spells marked **DAMAGE SPELL**. Place a dice in your 'Ward' slot with value 2 to show a ward is in play.

3RD LEVEL - WALL OF SORCERY
CRYSTALLINE WARD Target your sorcerer. Protects against Attack Actions and all spells marked **DAMAGE SPELL**. Place a dice in your 'Ward' slot with value 3 to show a ward is in play.

LORE OF MACHINATIONS

1ST LEVEL - WARPFLAME CAGE
MACHINATION SPELL Target an enemy tile with a single lesser daemon. Place a dice or token in the square status slot to indicate it is trapped until the start of your next turn.

2ND LEVEL - FLICKERING PRISON
MACHINATION SPELL Target an enemy tile with up to two lesser daemons. Place a dice or token in the square status slot to indicate they are trapped until the start of your next turn.

3RD LEVEL - CRYSTAL MAZE
MACHINATION SPELL Target an enemy tile with up to three lesser daemons. Place a dice or token in the square status slot to indicate they are trapped until the start of your next turn.

LORE OF DUPLICITY

1ST LEVEL - SUBTLE SUGGESTIONS
DUPLICITY SPELL Target an enemy tile. Roll a dice, on the score of 4+ a lesser daemon on that tile (chosen by the opposing player) becomes yours. Place it in an available slot on any of your tiles.

2ND LEVEL - SOUL SIPHON
DUPLICITY SPELL Target one of your own lesser daemons and inflict a wound upon it. Your sorcerer heals a wound.

3RD LEVEL - TREASON OF TZEENTCH
DUPLICITY SPELL Target an enemy tile. All the lesser daemons on the tile become yours. Place them on available slots in any of your tiles.

LORE OF FATE

1ST LEVEL - FICKLE CHANCE
DAMAGE SPELL Target an enemy tile or the enemy sorcerer. Inflict 1 wound and then roll a dice. On the score of 4+ generate a new dice for your destiny pool.

2ND LEVEL - LOCUS OF DESTINY
DAMAGE SPELL Target an enemy tile or the enemy sorcerer. Inflict D3 wounds then generate a new dice for your destiny pool.

3RD LEVEL - ARCHITECT OF FATE
DAMAGE SPELL Target an enemy tile or the enemy sorcerer. Inflict 3 wounds then generate a new dice for your destiny pool for each enemy model slain.

LORE OF CONFLAGRATION

1ST LEVEL - FIREBLAST
DAMAGE SPELL Target an enemy tile or the enemy sorcerer. Inflict D3 wounds.

2ND LEVEL - GREATER FIREBLAST
DAMAGE SPELL Target an enemy tile or the enemy sorcerer. Inflict D6 wounds.

3RD LEVEL - INFERNAL FLAMES
DAMAGE SPELL Target an enemy tile or the enemy sorcerer. Inflict 6 wounds. If you target a tile, it is set ablaze and no lesser daemons can be placed onto it (including from the 'Spilt' and 'Spit Again' rules). Place a dice or token in the square status slot. This effect remains in play until the start of your next turn.

LORE OF CONJURATION

1ST LEVEL - CONJURE BRIMSTONE HORRORS
CONJURATION SPELL Place D3 Brimstone Horrors on available slots in any of your tiles.

2ND LEVEL - CONJURE BLUE HORRORS
CONJURATION SPELL Place D3 Blue Horrors on available slots in any of your tiles.

3RD LEVEL - CONJURE PINK HORRORS
CONJURATION SPELL Place D3 Pink Horrors on available slots in any of your tiles.

LESSER DAEMONS

BRIMSTONE HORRORS

WOUNDS 1

BLUE HORRORS

WOUNDS 2

Split Again: If after a Spell or Attack Action has been resolved a Blue Horror has been slain, you may place a new Brimstone Horror on an available slot in the same tile.

PINK HORRORS

WOUNDS 2

Split: If after a Spell or Attack Action has been resolved a Pink Horror has been slain, you may place two new Blue Horrors on available slots in the same tile.

BLOOD BOWL
THE GAME OF FANTASY FOOTBALL

THE
DOOM LORDS
— TAKE TO THE FIELD! —

VENATOR BANDS

The underhive is infested with criminals, killers, deviants and worse, making it a rich hunting ground for the so-called 'Venator' bands – temporary coalitions of normally solitary Bounty Hunters. Here we present rules for using them in your games!

All across Necromunda, from the drudging halls of factorums and precinct blockhouse walls to the rusting gates of down-hive settlements and cross-tunnel gibbets, images of the faces of wanted fighters flutter in the stale breeze of the carbon scrubbers. A group of talented murderers can make a healthy living collecting these bounties, and with the promise of shared rewards and extra firepower they sometimes gather together into bands of ruthless professional killers. Drawn from every Clan, House and outland race on Necromunda, Venators come in all shapes and sizes – mixing ex-Goliath heavies and nimble Escher assassins, alongside disgraced watchmen or embittered, cast-out nobles. The most infamous are drawn from the ancient and much-feared Executioner Families, entire bloodlines founded on meting out the justice of Lord Helmawr. Most are sanctioned by the Guilders or the Imperial House itself and carry a hunter's oath-token. Many are not however, the Guilders often paying for the hunters' captives and kills all the same. Venator bands are not limited to Necromundans, and some even come from off world. Notorious abhuman Venators like the Brayhorn Boys or the Sons of Grindel are well known in certain reaches of the underhive, while some cloaked and cowled Venators have the hallmarks of xenos interlopers. In the underhive, lawmen don't ask too many questions if a masked killer dumps the corpse of a wanted ganger at their feet – they hand over the scrip and hope to the Emperor no one ever puts a price on their own head.

Venators are much feared throughout Necromundan society, their name invoked as a curse or cautionary warning. They hunt targets of all kinds, but the most lucrative, and indeed dangerous to hunt, are those of the population who have spontaneously come into psychic powers. So dangerous are these 'rogue psykers' that the Imperial House has issued an open contract on all of their kind. Only the most experienced Venator band would pursue such a foe, for they are wont to inadvertently unleash the power of the warp itself when cornered, but those that do – the so-called 'Venator Witch Hunters' – are amongst the most feared warriors of the hive cities. **OB/JTY**

THE RITES OF THE HUNT

Necromundan Bounty Hunters are a hugely varied class of individuals, ranging from desperadoes and gunslingers who hunt because they know no other way to earn the money to buy their next bottle of Wildsnake to witch hunters motivated as much by religious fervour as by wealth. Some border on being classified as death cults and are only allowed to exist so long as their murderous instincts serve the Imperial House.

The act of coming together into a Venator band is often a nigh-religious experience and one observed with much ritual. The oldest traditions still extant in the hives of Necromunda require the Bounty Hunters to set aside their individual identities for the duration of the hunt, donning hoods, snarling masks and occasionally the executioner's noose used as a symbol of faith across the hive world. When such Venators appear in a settlement, death is never far behind.

DESIGNER'S NOTES

Venator bands present an opportunity to let your gaming imagination run wild, a chance to use the Forge World Bounty Hunters in conjunction with a wide variety of models from the plastic gang sets and create a gang with a character all its own. The gang list presents a wide variety of profiles for each character type available, together with unprecedented access to a wide range of equipment thanks to them using almost the entire Trading Post as their equipment list. The options are almost limitless.

This is deliberate. Venators come from not only all corners of Necromunda, but from all corners of the Imperium and beyond. They are bands of bounty hunters thrown together by the knowledge that working in a group is far safer and more profitable in the long run than working alone. Former gang members, deserter guardsmen, abhumans, even aliens, all can be brought together within this unique gang, and over time just like any other gang it can become even more diverse and colourful through the addition of Hangers-on in the form of supporting staff, Exotic Beasts and so forth.

We would suggest that stat lines be chosen based on the character of the individual model you want to include, something which should also be considered when arming and equipping your fighters. Ask yourself how the stat line and weapons chosen work together, and does the stat line suit the character you'd imagine the model having?

When it comes to selecting the skill sets available to your Venator band, consider the overall character of the fighters. What is it that brings them together and what makes them work well as a team, what makes their leader a strong character that other ruthless cutthroats will follow? For all the individuals that make up the gang might be wildly different, the gang will function and feel better if careful consideration is given to the skills. This is the area in which the group identity really shines through.

VENATOR GANGS

GANG COMPOSITION

A Venator gang must follow these rules when it is founded and when new fighters are added to the gang:

- There must be one Hunt Leader (if the Leader is killed, see page 24 of Gang War).
- There can be no more than two Hunt Champions, plus one for every full 10 Reputation the band has – for example, a band with Reputation 24 could have up to four Hunt Champions.
- The total number of Hunters in the band must be equal to or higher than the total number of other fighters (Hunt Leaders and Hunt Champions) in the band, not counting Hangers-on.
- A fighter can be equipped with a maximum of five weapons. Only one weapon may have the Unwieldy Weapon Trait, and this counts as two weapons choices.
- Four profiles are presented for each category. When hiring a fighter one profile must be picked. It is possible to have several different profiles in a band – for example, a gang that includes three Hunt Champions could use a different Hunt Champion profile for each one.

HIERARCHY OF THE HUNT

Unless specified otherwise, a Venator Hunt Leader follows all of the rules for a Leader, and Hunt Champions follow all of the rules for Champions. For example, either one can lead a Group Activation – a Hunt Leader would be able to lead a group of two other fighters, while a Hunt Champion would be able to lead one other fighter. Should the Hunt Leader be killed, follow the rules for a Leader's death (see page 24 of Gang War One).

VENATORS IN CAMPAIGNS

Venator bands do not hold turf like other gangs in a campaign. They do not therefore gain or lose turf as a result of winning or losing battles and they can never hold any Special Territories.

They do however collect Income after the first battle of a cycle, but rather than multiplying their turf size by 10 they multiply their Reputation by 10 to determine the retainer they are paid by their patrons to continue operating in that area.

Additionally, the gang's Leader (and only the Leader) may make a special 'Work the Gang's Turf' action (see page 23 of Gang War) in the post-battle sequence to represent the Venators making an appeal to their patron for extra operating expenses. However, should the D6 roll be a 1 the plea has fallen on deaf ears and no extra funding is granted.

Finally, the Venators will earn additional income for every enemy fighter captured and not rescued, which they will automatically sell to the Guilders, and for any enemy fighters killed. When the Venators sell captives to the Guilders, they earn the full value of each fighter in credits rather than the usual half. When an opponent the Venators have just fought deletes a dead fighter from their roster during the Update Roster step of the post-battle sequence, the Venators immediately claim half of that fighter's value rounded up to the nearest 5 credits as bounty.

GAINING EXPERIENCE

Venators gain experience in the same way as any a normal House gang. Hunt Leaders and Hunt Champions can have their XP spent on Advancements, in the same way as a Leader or Champion. Hunters advance in the same way as Gangers and can become Specialists if a 2 or 12 is rolled for their Advancement.

SKILL ACCESS

When creating a Venator gang, pick any four skill sets apart from Leadership. Rank them from 1 to 4, 1 being the one that most embodies the way you envisage the band operates as a team. Each fighter's access to the skill sets is then determined by looking at the table below – this should be noted down separately.

	Primary	Secondary
Hunt Leader	1 & 2 plus leadership	3 & 4
Hunt Champion	1 & 2	3 & 4 plus leadership
Specialist	1 & 2	3 & 4

For example, Sarah is creating a Venator gang. She decides that their four skill sets, ranked in order, are: 1) Savvy, 2) Shooting, 3) Combat and 4) Agility. Her Hunt Leader's Primary skill sets are Savvy, Shooting and Leadership, and their Secondary skill sets are Combat and Agility. Her Specialist's Primary skill sets are Savvy and Shooting, and their Secondary skill sets are Combat and Agility.

HIRED GUNS AND DRAMATIS PERSONAE

Venator bands may hire Dramatis Personae and Hive Scum in the same way as other gangs, however they may not hire Bounty Hunters apart from Dramatis Personae ones (such as Grendl Grendlsen). This is because they are already a tightly knit group of bounty hunters themselves and are very reluctant to split profits with outsiders, but they will make use of local expertise where it suits their ends, and both Dramatis Personae and Hive Scum represent exactly this.

Additionally, Venator Bands may hire Hangers-on, but they use the following table:

Reputation	Maximum Hangers-on
Less than 9	0
10-14	1
15-19	2
20-24	3
Each additional 5	+1

> "Underhive law, for what it's worth, don't mean a thing to them and their kind. If there is a price on your head, no Guilder connections, uphive favours or gutter oaths are going to save your hide, because nothing, and I mean nothing, comes between a gang of Venators and their payday."
>
> Hallow Four-Fingers, Dustfalls Peacekeeper

FIGHTERS

A starting Venator gang is made up of the following fighters:

HUNT LEADER .... 105 CREDITS

Pick one of the following profiles to use when recruiting your Hunt Leader.

M	WS	BS	S	T	W	I	A	Ld	Cl	Wil	Int
5"	3+	3+	3	3	2	3+	2	7+	6+	6+	6+
3"	3+	4+	3	4	2	5+	2	6+	6+	5+	5+
4"	3+	5+	4	4	2	4+	2	7+	5+	8+	9+
4"	4+	2+	3	3	2	3+	1	5+	5+	6+	5+

EQUIPMENT LISTS:

A Venator Hunt Leader has no equipment. They may choose Common equipment and Rare equipment with a Rarity value up to and including 11 from the Trading Post. They have no equipment restrictions.

STARTING SKILL

Venator Hunt Leaders start with one skill chosen from their Primary skill sets.

HUNT CHAMPION ....80 CREDITS

Pick one of the following profiles to use when recruiting a Hunt Champion.

M	WS	BS	S	T	W	I	A	Ld	Cl	Wil	Int
5"	4+	4+	3	3	2	4+	2	7+	6+	7+	7+
3"	4+	4+	3	4	2	5+	2	6+	6+	6+	5+
4"	3+	5+	4	4	2	5+	2	7+	5+	8+	8+
4"	5+	2+	3	3	2	4+	1	6+	6+	6+	6+

EQUIPMENT:

A Venator Hunt Champion has no equipment. They may choose Common equipment and Rare equipment with a Rarity value up to and including 10 from the Trading Post. They have no equipment restrictions.

STARTING SKILL

Venator Hunt Champions start with one skill chosen from their Primary skill sets.

HUNTERS...45 CREDITS

Pick one of the following profiles to use when recruiting a Hunter.

M	WS	BS	S	T	W	I	A	Ld	Cl	Wil	Int
5"	4+	4+	3	3	1	4+	1	7+	6+	7+	7+
3"	4+	4+	3	4	1	5+	1	6+	6+	7+	6+
4"	3+	4+	3	4	1	5+	1	7+	6+	8+	9+
4"	5+	3+	3	3	1	4+	1	6+	6+	6+	7+

EQUIPMENT:

A Venator Hunter has no equipment. They may choose Common equipment and Rare equipment with a Rarity value up to and including 8 from the Trading Post. They can be equipped with Basic Weapons, Close Combat Weapons, Grenades, Pistols and Wargear.

HOUSE LEGACY: 20 CREDITS

(Goliath, Escher, Cawdor, Orlock, Van Saar, Delaque)

Bounty Hunters may be drawn to hunt from all over Necromunda and even beyond, and many exotic and outlandish countenances and accents are present in Venator gangs. But by far the most common bounty hunters on Necromunda are former gang members – a ganger may become a bounty hunter for many reasons – some are cast out by their House for some unforgivable indiscretion, others tire of taking orders from hated under-bosses, whilst still others desire more from life and break away from the confines of gang hierarchy in search of greater wealth and adventure.

Whatever the reason, such individuals will often cling to the trappings of their house identity, using weapons and armour commonly associated with their former house even as they rub shoulders with comrades who they once would have considered mortal enemies. Many even maintain close ties with former gang mates, keeping open valuable channels through which they retain access to specialist equipment and tap into insider information.

Should you wish, any fighter in a Venator gang may be given a single House Legacy for 20 credits. A fighter with a House Legacy may choose equipment from the Escher, Goliath, Van Saar, Delaque, Cawdor or Orlock House Equipment lists. For example, a Hunt Champion with the Goliath House Legacy may take Furnace Plate armour and a 'Krumper' Rivet Cannon should they wish, or any other item from the House Goliath Equipment list, exclusive or otherwise, at the cost shown there.

There is no restriction on House Legacies, a Venator gang may contain as many or as few as you wish. However each fighter may only originate from one house!

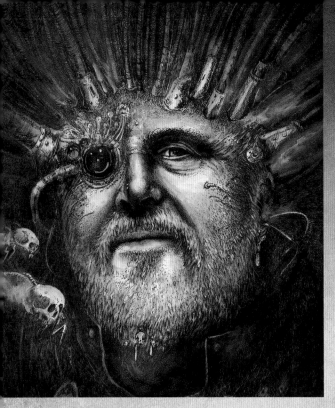

BLANCHITSU

For over three decades John Blanche has shaped the worlds of Warhammer with his evocative artwork. His style has enthused and excited many painters and modellers, and Blanchitsu is our regular feature celebrating John's dark, gothic visions and their influence. This month, we delve into the bizarre world of the Tor Megiddo.

This month's journey into the world of Blanchitsu led us to Helsinki (the capital of Finland, not the sister hive city of Helsreach, and it was mostly by email, but anyway) where a very unusual-looking game was being played by a keen group of hobbyists, all who had been influenced by John's work. Over the last few months they worked tirelessly to create warbands for their game – the Tor Megiddo project – and in the coming issues we'll be showcasing their impressive creations. Alexander Winberg and Alexander Lunde – two of the chaps behind the Tor Megiddo project – explain what it's all about.

"Tor Megiddo is a setting created by Helge Dahl and myself," says Alexander Winberg. "It is a post-apocalyptic hive world that, through over-exploitation, has been reduced to a radioactive desert. Now, warbands and tribes scrape a living from the ruined earth, desperate to find traces of promethium that linger beneath the surface."

"I wanted to build something grand and lumbering for this game – a moving scenery piece," says Alexander Lunde, who created the Promethium Tower – the objective for all the warbands in the Tor Megiddo game. "I reckoned that because of the scarcity of promethium and the nomadic tribes inhabiting the world, the promethium rigs would also have to move. Some are controlled by the tribes or warbands, others walk free." You can see Alexander's Promethium Tower to the right and his warband – the Vortrekkers – over the page, followed closely by Alexander Winberg's warband, the 66 Fangs. Enjoy!

Many people that emulate John's style are inspired by his evocative artwork. This classic piece from the front cover of the Dark Future novel *Ghost Dancers* by Brian Craig was painted by John many years ago – it, and pieces like it, heavily influenced the models in this project.

The Promethium Tower was created by Alexander Lunde – it is the prize that all the warbands are fighting for. A vast walking machine, Alexander built it using the legs of an Imperial Knight, parts from the Sector Mechanicus and a Sigmarite Mausoleum.

BLANCHITSU

THE VORTREKKERS BY ALEXANDER LUNDE

"Sent out by one of the mighty Rust Lords of Tor Megiddo, the Vortrekkers seek one of the vast promethium towers that roam the wastes," says Alexander. "Led by a local guide, they now have eyes on one of the tors." Alexander's warband includes an impressive war machine known as the Rust Beetle.

Alexander made good use of the Genestealer Cults kits for his gang members. The leader of the gang is Omic **(1)** who, like all his warriors, wears a reflective glarehelm to protect him from the harsh sun and radioactive dust of Tor Megiddo. The model is based on a Hybrid Neophyte with arms from a Tempestus Scion and a chainblade from a Tartaros Terminator.

Kluntz the Old **(2)** controls the warband's scrap servitor and carries a seismic totem – a powerful explosive device. He is also converted from a Neophyte, with arms and gun taken from a Skitarii Ranger.

Yibal **(3)** carries a Megiddo-pattern chainsaw. Like all the models in Alexander's warband, Yibal is painted in drab and dusty oranges, yellows and beiges, not only to reflect the world these warriors fight on, but to show their allegiance to their Rust Lord.

Cwm **(4)** carries a welding lance – a tool he has used as a weapon on many occasions. The lance is converted from an Imperial Guard flamer. Note the metal totems that hang from his helm.

1

2

3

4

The Guide **(5)** leads the Vortrekkers in their quest to find the Promethium Tower. She is converted from a Ruststalker's torso combined with an old Bretonnian model's legs.

The Flesh Dervish **(6)** was acquired by the Vortrekkers from a mutant oilclan. It is converted from a Plaguebearer with bionic limbs from various Skitarii kits.

The Rust Beetle **(7)** accompanies the Vortrekkers. Alexander built it using the torso of an Imperial Knight and the legs of an Onager Dunecrawler with the addition of Sector Mechanicus bits. The gunner Burgan sits in the crow's nest.

5

6

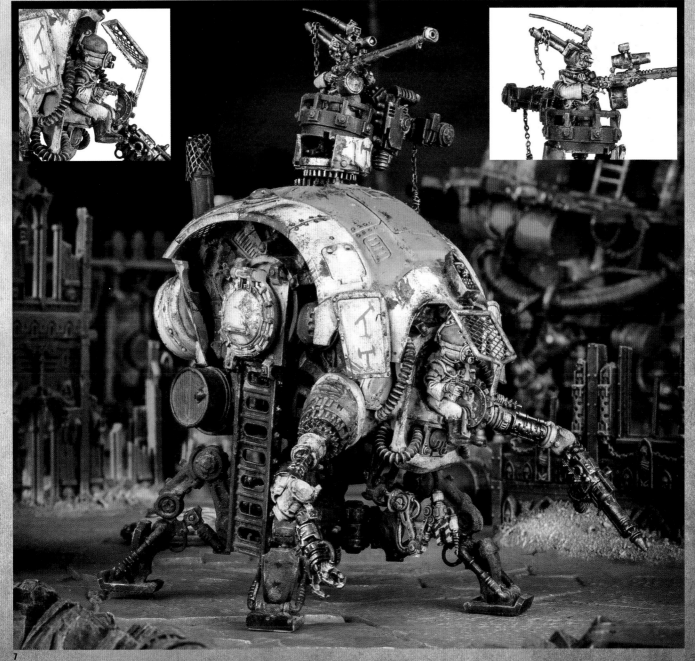

7

THE 66 FANGS BY ALEXANDER WINBERG

"The members of my warband all have some sort of protective gear on, and their styles differ since they have to scavenge and rebuild it," says Alexander. "When painting my warband, I wanted to show the harsh conditions they are forced to deal with. They live in a cruel world and can't afford the luxury of art and decoration. Dust is everywhere and nothing's clean. I also used a lot of weathering pigments – it was a new technique for me and I enjoyed experimenting with them."

1

Blue Ruin (1) is the leader of Alexander's warband and the ruler of Death Valley. "I wanted Blue Ruin to be heavily armoured – an important consideration in the wastelands," says Alexander. "She is clad in heavy plate armour, except for her arms and head. She lost her right arm a long time ago in a battle with rad mutants, thus her bionic arm. She is armed with a chainsword, a slug pistol and a heavy duty shotgun." Blue Ruin is converted using the shoulder guards from Mannfred von Carstein, a Daemonette's head and an Ork bike. Her bionic arm is from a Skitarii Ruststalker.

Steel Tomahawk (2) is a member of the Kong Elite – a group of warriors that have been sent to fight alongside Blue Ruin. He is converted from a Chaos Warrior with the head of a Genestealer Cults Neophyte Hybrid and a hot-shot volley gun from the Tempestus Scions.

Black Acid (3) is another member of the Kong Elite. He is converted from an old Chaos Forsaken model with arms from a Tempestus Scion and a backpack from the Ork Boyz kit. His head (complete with cracked visor) comes from the Neophyte Hybrids set.

2

3

"Zogg the Flesh Baron **(4)** is a guide that has promised to show the way into the Promethean Tower and the seas of promethium it is said to hold. But it is all lies and he seeks to betray the 66 Fangs." He is converted from a Putrid Blightking with the head of a Kataphron Breacher and a chainblade taken from a Sentinel.

'Fresh' Scars is a scout in the 66 Fangs warband **(5)**. He has been converted from the Imperial Space Marine miniature that came out a couple of years ago, with a Space Marine head and a backpack from an Ork Loota.

"Thirteen, Daughter of Misery **(6)** is a member of the 66 Fangs. She is also a member of the elite warrior lodge, the Kong. Her role in the warband is to provide heavy support and she wields a heavy stubber that should come in handy when dealing with any large threats. She is based on Slambo the Chaos Warrior, which I converted to look like a techno-barbarian. She has a very dark paint job with a limited palette – I hope this helps bring across her dark and pessimistic nature."

Iron Moon **(7)** is the driver of the Firecracker **(8)**. She is converted from a Khorne Bloodbound model with the head from a Sicarian Ruststalker. The Firecracker is a Taurox converted with wheels from an Ork Trukk.

4

5

6

7

8

THE WAR FOR TOR MEGIDDO CONTINUES

The Land shakes beneath the fury of the storm.

The sand is drenched in blood and oil.

Most holy Promethium, it fills our veins with wrath.

Ride forth, warlord! Blessed by the Cog and the Bolt!

Wage war in the sun!

Can you hear the engines starting?

Can you feel the boiling blood?

Can you see the storm approaching?

War in the sun.

Come back next month to see more of the Tor Megiddo project – the Promethium Tower awaits you! **DH**

PAINT SPLATTER

Paint Splatter is our regular feature on painting Citadel miniatures. Each month we present stage-by-stage guides to painting your miniatures, and all the information you need to make use of them. This month: Idoneth Deepkin and Chaos Chosen teams in Blood Bowl!

READ THIS FIRST: HOW TO USE THIS GUIDE

Over the following pages you'll find stage-by-stage painting guides for some of the latest new releases. These painting guides, combined with the information on these pages, tells you everything you need to know to paint your models just like the ones you can see in the example photos. Each guide begins with an example photo, showing all the parts of the model. You'll then find stage-by-stage guides to painting each of these areas, as shown to the right.

FLESH
SILVER ARMOUR
BRASS
WEAPON HANDLE
TROUSERS
TASSELS
CLOTH
BOOTS/LEATHER
CLOTH TRIM

Stage Name: The part of the model you'll be painting in this step, as shown in the example photo.

Stage Number: Each part is painted in a number of stages. Simply follow them in order.

Stage Photo: This shows exactly what has been done at this stage – use the picture to see where to apply the colours and what they should look like. Use the example photo to identify similar areas of the model and paint these at the same time.

FLESH
4
Layer: Pallid Wych Flesh
S Layer

Technique: There's more than one way to put paint on a model. Here's our advice on which technique to use for each stage – in this case, a layer. You can read about all of these techniques on the opposite page.

Paint Name: The Citadel paint used for this stage. In this case, it's Pallid Wych Flesh (which is a Layer paint). You can read more about the Citadel range of paints below.

Brush: The Citadel brush used for this stage – the name here is exactly what you'll find on the brush – in this case, an S Layer brush – making it easy to identify the right one. You can read more about brushes below.

CITADEL PAINTS

CITADEL BASE
LEADBELCHER

Base paints contain a high concentration of pigment. These strong colours are the ideal foundation for painting. Some Base paints are available as sprays.

CITADEL SHADE
CASANDORA YELLOW

Shades are much thinner than other paints, formulated to flow into recesses, providing natural, effective shading and help to define details on your miniatures.

CITADEL LAYER
EMPEROR'S CHILDREN

Layer paints are used to create highlights on a miniature. Formulated to be slightly translucent, they can be applied over Base paints and each other with great results.

CITADEL DRY
KINDLEFLAME

Dry paints are designed to make drybrushing as straightforward as possible. They are formulated to a much thicker consistency than other paints.

CITADEL EDGE
DECHALA LILAC

Edge paints help to give your miniatures a final sharp, bright highlight. The paints possess the same formulation as the Layer paints, but with a much lighter tone.

CITADEL TEXTURE
ASTROGRANITE

Texture paints provide a textured finish – either a granular, sandy effect or a hard, dry, cracked earth one – perfect for painting the bases of your miniatures.

CITADEL TECHNICAL
LAHMIAN MEDIUM

Technical paints are designed to help you achieve a range of effects, from rust and corrosion to foetid slurry and bloody gore, adding an extra level of realism.

CITADEL SPRAYS

Two Citadel sprays – Corax White and Chaos Black – are available, designed specially for undercoating your models. Some Base paints are also available as sprays, allowing you to basecoat whole models quickly and easily. Be careful when spraying your models and always read the instructions. Be sure to shake the can for a couple of minutes before use and always spray in short bursts from a distance of 20 to 30cm for the best results.

CITADEL MACRAGGE BLUE MODEL PAINT

CITADEL BRUSHES

There are seventeen brushes in the Citadel paint brush range and all of them have specific uses when painting miniatures.

BASE BRUSHES
The Base brushes (in sizes – S, M, L and XL) have hard-wearing bristles designed to hold plenty of paint. With a flat shape and a top edge, you can use them side-on for greater coverage, or use the edge for more control.

SHADE BRUSHES
Shade brushes (M and L) are designed to soak up a large amount of paint in their bristles so you can apply lots of a Shade in one go. These are perfect for applying washes over the whole of a miniature quickly and easily.

LAYER BRUSHES
Layer brushes are ideal for building up layers and highlights. Choose the right size of brush for the job (M or S). Artificer Layer brushes (XS, S and M) are extra high-quality brushes ideal for the most careful painting of the smallest details.

DRY BRUSHES
There are three Dry brushes in the range – S, M and L. They are made of ox hair and synthetic fibres that enable them to survive the rigours of swift drybrushing. The flat profile provides consistent coverage on raised areas.

GLAZE BRUSHES
Glaze brushes are similar to Shade brushes but with a smaller head. They are ideal for applying glazes – washes of colour to add vibrancy – to particular areas of a model. You can also use a Glaze brush to apply Shades to small areas.

UNDERCOAT

Applying an undercoat before your basecoat will improve the coverage and effectiveness of later layers, especially if basecoating with a brush rather than a spray. Most people use a Corax White or Chaos Black undercoat spray.

THE CITADEL PAINT APP

Before you start painting, we recommend you download the Citadel Paint App. You can find it on the Google Play Store and the Apple App Store. The Citadel Paint App includes guides to producing more than 100 different colour schemes, which you can browse by colour or by miniature, and you can use the Inventory and Wishlist features to keep track of the paints you need for your latest project. Throughout Paint Splatter, you'll find 'On the App' boxes, where we point you to alternative colour schemes you can use on the miniatures featured in this month's issue for even more options when painting your models.

WARHAMMER TV

Every day Warhammer TV offers new videos featuring top tips and painting guides, including videos for all the techniques you'll see used in Paint Splatter. You can find Warhammer TV online at:

youtube.com/
WarhammerTV

THE CITADEL PAINTING SYSTEM: TECHNIQUES

With the Citadel Painting System, you can choose the colours you want to paint your models, select the appropriate technique for each stage, and apply them quickly and easily. Here's how to do it.

BASECOAT

A well-applied basecoat makes for a strong foundation for later stages. Citadel Base paints are specially formulated for the job. If basecoating with a brush, thin the paint with a little water and apply several thin coats for even coverage.

SPRAY

If your miniatures are predominantly one colour, it's much quicker to use a spray to basecoat them. Mount your models on a stick with some double-sided tape before spraying. For the best results, spray in short, controlled bursts. Always read the instructions.

LAYER

Layering helps bring out the detail on a model. By applying progressively lighter layers of colour, you can create realistic highlights on a model. Apply layers in thin coats – you can always apply a second thin coat if you need to.

EDGE HIGHLIGHT

A final bright highlight brings out the very finest details on a model and really helps it stand out on the tabletop. For these edge highlights, apply the layer only to the most raised areas. It's often easier to use the edge of the brush for this job, rather than the tip.

WASH

Applying a wash is an easy way to bring out subtle details and textures on a model. Citadel Shades are specially formulated for this, as they will run into the recesses on a model and create effective shading with minimal effort.

ALL-OVER WASH

When you apply a wash over a whole area or model, most will run into the recesses but some will dry over the whole area, providing all over shading. Apply these all-over washes early, over the basecoat or first layer, to avoid too much tidying-up later on.

RECESS WASH

Sometimes you will want to focus a wash in the recesses, leaving the surface colour as it is. For these recess washes, use a smaller brush (an M Glaze is ideal) and carefully apply the wash directly into the recesses. Once dry, you can tidy up around it if needed.

DRYBRUSH

Drybrushing is a way to capture raised details and create natural highlights quickly. To drybrush, load a brush with paint and then wipe most of it off on a paper towel, then flick the almost dry bristles across the model to catch the raised areas.

OVERBRUSH

Overbrushing is used to apply paint quickly to large areas of a model, while avoiding the recesses. This allows you to apply layers of colour quickly with the recesses providing shading. The technique is the same as drybrushing but with more paint on the brush.

GLAZES

Glazing is an advanced technique that some painters use to intensify an area of colour or unify layers of highlights where they are a bit too stark. A glaze is usually the final stage in painting a particular area and works by adding a translucent layer of colour.

IDONETH DEEPKIN NAMARTI THRALL

The Namarti are the lowest and most populous caste of the Idoneth Deepkin. In this painting guide, we show you how to paint a Namarti Thrall. You can use these same stages for your Namarti Reavers, too. The model was painted over a Corax White spray undercoat and the flesh was painted using the new Ionrach Skin and Deepkin Flesh paints. If you haven't already, be sure to pick these paints up with your models!

LIGHT WASHES

The pale, otherworldly look for the Thrall's flesh was achieved by using light washes, where the Shade (in this case, Drakenhof Nightshade) is thinned with Lahmian Medium before being applied to the model. This means that while the wash will still flow into the recesses and provide natural shading, it will alter the underlying basecoat less than a heavier wash would, for a lighter tone overall. The same was done on the cloth, this time with Nuln Oil. If used straight out of the pot, Nuln Oil would be too dark for the teal and blue-grey of the cloth and trim; thinning it with Lahmian Medium means it still provides some nice, deep shading, but adds a lighter, more grey tone to the raised areas.

SILVER ARMOUR
FLESH
BRASS
TASSELS
WEAPON HANDLE
CLOTH
TROUSERS
BOOTS/LEATHER
CLOTH TRIM

	FLESH	CLOTH	CLOTH TRIM	SILVER ARMOUR	TASSELS
READY FOR BATTLE Most Idoneth Deepkin armies feature several units of Namarti, meaning you may have quite a few models to paint. If you want to get your Namarti onto the battlefield as quickly as possible, we recommend the 'Ready for Battle' approach. What that means is painting your models in a couple of simple stages (usually a basecoat and a wash on each of the main areas) and then basing up the model ready to play a game with. Even with just these basic colours, whole units of models will look great, and the sense of being able to 'finish' your models and get playing with them quickly can be a great motivator. You can always come back and add more stages later if you want.	 **1** Basecoat: Ionrach Skin — M Base	 **1** Basecoat: Thousand Sons Blue — M Base	 **1** Basecoat: Fenrisian Grey — L Base	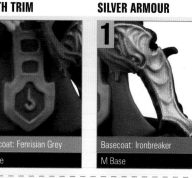 **1** Basecoat: Ironbreaker — M Base	 **1** Basecoat: Wild Rider Red — M Base
	 **2** Wash: Drakenhof Nightshade & Lahmian Medium (1:1) — M Shade	 **2** Wash: Nuln Oil/Lahmian Medium 1:1 — M Shade	 **2** Wash: Nuln Oil/Lahmian Medium 1:1 — M Shade	 **2** Wash: Coelia Greenshade — M Shade	 **2** Wash: Carroburg Crimson — M Shade
TAKING IT FURTHER There's a saying that "A model is only finished when you decide it is." This is a principle worth remembering since it means not only can you have the benefits of getting your models painted Ready for Battle quickly and easily, but you can also return to them at your leisure and take things further.	 **3** Layer: Deepkin Flesh — M Layer	 **3** Layer: Ahriman Blue — M Layer	 **3** Layer: Fenrisian Grey (Tidy-up) — M Layer	 **3** Layer: Runefang Steel — M Layer	 **3** Layer: Fire Dragon Bright — M Layer
These extra touches can be as many or as few as you like – you can apply the stages shown here selectively; you don't have to use all of them. Highlighting the flesh (stages 3 and 4), for example, will make a big difference to the model, so you might well decide that's enough.	 **4** Layer: Pallid Wych Flesh — S Layer	 **4** Layer: Temple Guard Blue — S Layer	 **4** Layer: Blue Horror — S Layer	 **4** Glaze: Guilliman Blue — M Glaze	 **4** Layer: Ungor Flesh — S Layer

CREATURES OF THE DEEP

The Idoneth Deepkin range includes a huge number of nightmarish creatures as extras in the kits (you can see even more of these in Designers' Notes, on page 28, and 'Eavy Metal, on page 36). These make great additions to the bases of your models, some additional variety. Here's one example, painted in a light orange to contrast with the deep blue and pale flesh of the rest of the Namarti Thralls. As this is a small piece, for ease of painting it was 'basecoated' using glazes and washes straight over Corax White.

1

Undercoat: Corax White
Spray

2

Wash: Fuegan Orange
Wash: Guilliman Blue
M Glaze

3

Layer: Fire Dragon Bright
Layer: Waywatcher Green
M Layer

4

Layer: Tau Light Ochre
Layer: Abaddon Black (eye)
S Layer

THINNING SHADES

Thinning Shades with Lahmian Medium means the consistency remains the same, unlike using water, which will cause the washes to become runnier. Simply combine your Shade with Lahmian Medium on a palette in the suggested ratios. So for 1:1, add one brushful of Lahmian Medium to one brushful of (in this example) Nuln Oil. You can see the unthinned Shade beside it for comparison.

BOOTS/LEATHER	TROUSERS	BRASS	WEAPON HANDLES	WEAPON HANDLES
1  Basecoat: Rhinox Hide — M Base	**1**  Basecoat: Incubi Darkness — M Base	**1**  Basecoat: Fulgurite Copper — M Base	**1**  Basecoat: Khorne Red — M Base	**1**  Basecoat: Leadbelcher — M Base
2  Wash: Nuln Oil — M Shade	**2**  Wash: Nuln Oil — M Shade	**2**  Wash: Reikland Fleshshade — M Shade	**2**  Wash: Nuln Oil — M Shade	**2**  Wash: Nuln Oil — M Shade
3  Layer: Doombull Brown — M Layer	**3**  Layer: Kabalite Green — M Layer	**3**  Layer: Liberator Gold — M Layer		**3**  Layer: Ironbreaker — S Layer
4  Layer: Skrag Brown — S Layer	**4**  Layer: Nurgling Green — S Layer	**4** 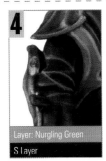 Layer: Stormhost Silver — S Layer		

NAMARTI THRALL: READY FOR BATTLE

This Namarti Thrall has been painted using stages 1 and 2 for each area and then based up, ready to play a game with. Quick and easy! Painting all the basecoats together allows areas like the cloth and trim (which use the same wash) to be washed at the same time.

NAMARTI THRALL: FURTHER STAGES

Later, the model was taken further using stages 3 and 4 of this painting guide. Remember, you don't have to do this all at once – you can add extra stages to different areas as and when you have time. As you can see, the final result is absolutely stunning.

MODELLING AND PAINTING

ARMY PAINTERS
The Studio's Army Painters are the team who paint many of the armies you see in the pages of rulebooks, battletomes, codexes and White Dwarf. As well as painting these inspirational collections of miniatures, the Army Painters are also the folks responsible for producing the stage-by-stage painting guides that we feature in Paint Splatter each month. The members of the team are: Tom Moore, Paul Norton, Jay Goldfinch and Dan Hyams. This month, Forge World's Giuseppe Chiafele also contributed a Blood Bowl painting guide.

IDONETH DEEPKIN AKHELIAN KING

The Akhelian King is an impressive hero model and one of the leaders of the army, so Jay from the Studio's Army Painting team really went to town on this example. Character models like the Akhelian King are well worth spending a little extra time and attention on, but remember you don't need to do that all in one go. Even on a model like this, you can still follow the Ready for Battle principle (discussed on page 122) or take some stages from the Namarti Thrall painting guide if you want. Whatever your approach, on a model like this you will want to paint the largest areas (like the flesh, scales and cloak) first.

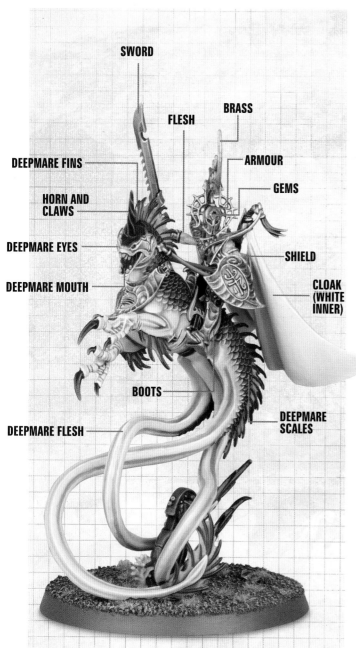

- SWORD
- FLESH
- BRASS
- ARMOUR
- GEMS
- DEEPMARE FINS
- HORN AND CLAWS
- DEEPMARE EYES
- SHIELD
- DEEPMARE MOUTH
- CLOAK (WHITE INNER)
- BOOTS
- DEEPMARE SCALES
- DEEPMARE FLESH

DEEPMARE FLESH

1 Basecoat: Rakarth Flesh
M Base

2 Wash: Reikland Fleshshade
M Shade

3 Layer: Rakarth Flesh (Tidy-up)
M Layer

4 Layer: Pallid Wych Flesh
M Layer

5 Layer: White Scar
S Layer

DEEPMARE SCALES

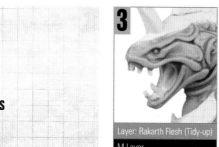

1 Basecoat: Khorne Red
S Base

2 Wash: Druchii Violet
M Glaze

3 Layer: Evil Sunz Scarlet
S Layer

4 Layer: Fire Dragon Bright
S Layer

DEEPMARE MOUTH

1 Basecoat: Screamer Pink
S Base

2 Wash: Druchii Violet
S Glaze

3 Layer: Pink Horror
S Layer

4 Basecoat: Rhinox Hide (teeth)
S Base

5 Layer: Balor Brown
S Layer

6 Layer: Screaming Skull
S Layer

DEEPMARE FLESH

To keep the Deepmare's flesh suitably pale, don't let the Reikland Fleshshade wash overpower the Rakarth Flesh basecoat. You can apply the wash heavily on the head for definition but on the rest of the body try thinning it with a little Lahmian Medium, or apply just a little Shade and use your brush to work it evenly over the whole area.

DEEPMARE SCALES

While the red of the scales contrasts with the pale flesh, the effect will be more natural if there's a gradual transition (rather than a hard line) between the two. To do this, thin down the Khorne Red basecoat and apply it almost like a wash. You can build it up more heavily with extra coats on the areas further away from the flesh.

CITADEL PAINT ON THE APP

DEEPMARE COLOURS
The Deepmare offers an opportunity to add some different colours to your army. Here's some suggestions for colour schemes you could use on the scales.

 Blue

 Dark Orange

 Emerald Green

 Dark Purple

DEEPMARE FINS

1 Basecoat: Fuegan Orange
M Base

2 Basecoat: Khorne Red (spines)
M Layer

3 Layer: Xereus Purple (tips)
M Layer

4 Layer: Warpfriend Grey
S Layer

HORN AND CLAWS

1 Basecoat: Incubi Darkness
M Base

2 Wash: Nuln Oil
M Shade

3 Layer: Kabalite Green
S Layer

4 Layer: Ogryn Camo
S Layer

DEEPMARE EYES

1 Basecoat: Abaddon Black
M Layer

2 Layer: Temple Guard Blue
S Layer

3 Layer: Abaddon Black (dot)
S Layer

FLESH

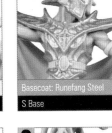
1 Basecoat: Flayed One Flesh
M Base

2 Wash: Reikland Fleshshade
M Shade

3 Layer: Flayed One Flesh
M Layer

4 Layer: Pallid Wych Flesh
S Layer

ARMOUR

1 Basecoat: Runefang Steel
S Base

2 Wash: Coelia Greenshade
M Glaze

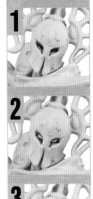
3 Glaze: Guilliman Blue
M Glaze

4 Layer: Stormhost Silver
S Layer

GLAZING THE ARMOUR

A glaze of Guilliman Blue is used on the Akhelian King's armour. The key is to apply the glaze selectively. The armour has a bright silver sheen, with a green tinge to it from the wash of Coelia Greenshade. Focus the Guilliman Blue around the thickest bands of armour for a sea-like blue-green effect.

EYES

Paint the flesh around the eyes first, before basecoating the eyes themselves with Rhinox Hide (**1**). Next, apply a layer of White Scar, leaving some Rhinox Hide around the edges (**2**). Finally, add a small dot of Abaddon Black (**3**).

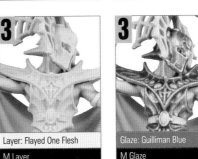
1

2

3

CHOOSING SHADES

Most colours have a natural Shade associated with them – Nuln Oil for silver, Carroburg Crimson for reds and so on – but you can produce really interesting effects by changing your choice of Shade and there are some great examples of that on this Akhelian King, such as the use of Coelia Greenshade on both the silver armour and the brass shield. Why not try out a few different combinations on some test models?

EMBLEMS

The Akhelian King's cloak features an elaborate emblem. This is actually part of the trim so can be painted at the same time using the same stages. The one thing you may want to do is basecoat the emblem and the trim before painting the rest of the cloak so you don't get any of the basecoat on the blue parts once you've already finished them.

SUB-ASSEMBLY SECRETS

The Akhelian King was painted in several parts, known as sub-assemblies. It's up to you whether or not you want to follow this method, and how many parts to keep separate, but the principle remains the same – mount each sub-assembly on a spare base or flying stand for ease of handling and cover the points where you'll later need to glue the model together with a little adhesive putty before spraying or painting the model – plastic glue won't stick the model together if a layer of paint gets in the way.

'EAVY METAL

Want to find out how the 'Eavy Metal team painted the Idoneth Deepkin's monstrous mounts? Turn to page 36 for 'Eavy Metal Masterclass!

CLOAK

Painting cloth can be tricky but you'll get great results by doing on two things: carefully applying the washes just to the recesses (and, in the case, just on the uppermost parts of the cloak, as you can see in the pictures) and painting your highlights neatly along the raised folds, with each layer a little narrower than the one before.

GEMS

Small details like gems can really enhance a centrepiece model like this if given a bit of extra attention. To paint them as shown here, apply each layer over a progressively smaller part of the gem, and finish with a single small dot of White Scar towards the top. If you prefer, you can use of the Gemstone paints for a quick alternative.

CLOAK (BLUE OUTER)

1 Basecoat: Thousand Sons Blue
L Base

2 Wash (Recess): Nuln Oil
M Shade

3 Layer: Thousand Sons Blue
M Layer

4 Layer: Ahriman Blue
S Layer

5 Layer: Temple Guard Blue
S Layer

CLOAK TRIM

1 Basecoat: Fenrisian Grey
S Base

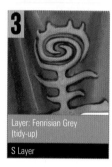
2 Wash (Recess): Nuln Oil
S Glaze

3 Layer: Fenrisian Grey (tidy-up)
S Layer

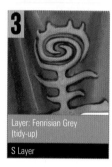
4 Layer: Blue Horror
S Layer

CLOAK (WHITE INNER)

1 Basecoat: Celestra Grey
M Base

2 Wash (Recess) Nuln Oil
M Shade

3 Layer: Ulthuan Grey
M Layer

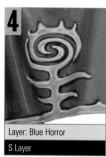
4 Layer: White Scar
S Layer

TROUSERS

1 Basecoat: Incubi Darkness
S Base

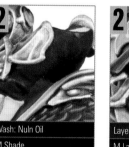
2 Wash: Nuln Oil
M Shade

3 Layer: Incubi Darkness (tidy-up)
M Layer

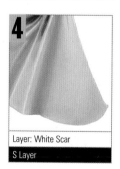
4 Layer: Kabalite Green
S Layer

5 Layer: Nurgling Green
S Layer

BOOTS

1 Basecoat: Rhinox Hide
S Base

2 Layer: Doombull Brown
M Layer

3 Layer: Skrag Brown
M Layer

4 Layer: Deathclaw Brown
S Layer

GEMS

1
Basecoat: Abaddon Black
M Layer

2
Layer: Mephiston Red
S Layer

3
Layer: Troll Slayer Orange
S Layer

4
Layer: Yriel Yellow
S Layer

5
Layer: White Scar (dot)
XS Artificer Layer

6
Layer: 'Ardcoat
M Glaze

BRASS

1
Basecoat: Fulgurite Copper
M Base

2
Wash: Reikland Fleshshade
M Shade

3
Layer: Liberator Gold
M Layer

4
Layer: Stormhost Silver
S Layer

SWORD

1
Basecoat: Ironbreaker
M Base

2
Wash: Drakenhof Nightshade
M Shade

3
Layer: Ironbreaker
M Layer

4
Layer: Stormhost Silver
S Layer

SHIELD

1
Basecoat: Runelord Brass
L Base

2
Wash: Coelia Greenshade
M Glaze

3
Layer: Runelord Bass (tidy-up)
M Layer

4
Layer: Stormhost Silver
S Layer

SWORD HILT

1
Basecoat: Khorne Red
S Base

2
Wash (Recess): Nuln Oil
S Layer

3
Layer: Evil Sunz Scarlet
S Layer

4
Layer: Fire Dragon Bright
S Layer

GEMSTONE PAINTS

Gemstone paints are Technical paints that create a gem-like effect. To do this, first paint the gem with your choice of metallic paint (Runefang Steel or Retributor Armour, for example) and when it's dry paint over it with your chosen gem paint – Soulstone Blue, Waystone Green or Spiritstone Red. In the example below (from a Kharadron Overlords skyvessel), the gem was first painted with a basecoat of Retributor Armour **(1)** before being allowed to dry and then given a coat of Waystone Green, one of the Gemstone paints **(2)**.

1
Layer: Retributor Armour
M Base

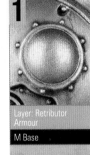

2
Layer: Waystone Green
M Glaze

BASING: STONE AND CORAL

The Idoneth Deepkin miniatures give you the option of a lot of different modelling elements on their bases that you can make use of if you want. On the Akhelian King, the base features a large stone bearing Idoneth runes, as you can see below. You can find the colours for this to the right. We recommend painting the stone separately from the model as that way you can undercoat it with Mechanicus Standard Grey spray to save time.

STONE
Basecoat: Mechanicus Standard Grey
Citadel Spray paint

Wash: Agrax Earthshade
M Shade

Drybrush: Mechanicus Standard Grey
L Dry

Drybrush: Karak Stone
L Dry

Drybrush: Screaming Skull
L Dry

STONE INLAY
Basecoat: Pallid Wych Flesh
S Base

Wash: Seraphim Sepia
M Glaze

Layer: Pallid Wych Flesh
M Layer

Layer: White Scar
S Layer

CORAL
Basecoat: Baharroth Blue
S Base

Glaze: Guilliman Blue
M Glaze

Glaze: Waywatcher Green
M Glaze

Drybrush: Ulthuan Grey
S Dry

BARNACLES
Basecoat: Rakarth Flesh
M Layer

Wash: Seraphim Sepia
M Glaze

Layer: Pallid Wych Flesh
S Layer

MODELLING AND PAINTING

BASECOATS AND WASHES
For these models, we suggest applying all the basecoats first and then doing all of the washes at the same time, as several areas on both models share an Agrax Earthshade wash.

THE DOOM LORDS CHAOS CHOSEN BLOOD BOWL TEAM

The Doom Lords are one of the most famed Chaos teams in the Blood Bowl world and their red, black and gold colours are iconic. You can recreate them for yourself using this handy painting guide! Although Chaos Chosen teams feature both Chaos Warriors and Beastmen, the palette used across the two doesn't vary all that much, so you can safely batch paint your whole team as one if that's your preferred method. Both types of player share the red and black armour, the leather and the gold, while even the two skin tones, the horns and the fur share an Agrax Earthshade wash, so painting all together should prove quick and efficient.

RED ARMOUR

1 Basecoat: Mephiston Red — S Base

2 Wash: Agrax Earthshade — M Glaze

3 Layer: Evil Sunz Scarlet — M Layer

4 Layer: Wild Rider Red — S Layer

5 Layer: Tau Light Ochre — XS Artificer Layer

BLACK

1 Basecoat: Abaddon Black — S Base

2 Wash: Druchii Violet — M Glaze

3 Layer: Dark Reaper — M Layer

4 Layer: Fenrisian Grey — S Layer

5 Layer: Ceramite White — XS Artificer Layer

LEATHER

1 Basecoat: Rhinox Hide — S Base

2 Wash: Agrax Earthshade — M Glaze

3 Layer: Skrag Brown — S Layer

4 Layer: Balor Brown — XS Artificer Layer

METAL

1 Basecoat: Ironbreaker — M Base

2 Wash: Nuln Oil — M Glaze

3 Layer: Ironbreaker — S Layer

4 Layer: Runefang Steel — XS Artificer Layer

SKIN

1
Basecoat: Cadian Fleshtone
M Base

2
Wash: Agrax Earthshade
M Shade

3
Layer: Kislev Flesh
M Layer

4
Layer: Flayed One Flesh
S Layer

GOLD

1
Basecoat: Retributor Armour
S Base

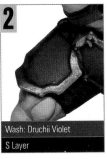

2
Wash: Druchii Violet
S Layer

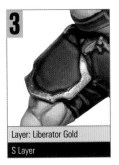

3
Layer: Liberator Gold
S Layer

4
Layer: Runefang Steel
XS Artificer Layer

BEASTMAN SKIN

1
Basecoat: Rhinox Hide
M Base

2
Wash: Agrax Fleshshade
M Shade

3
Layer: Mournfang Brown
M Layer

4
Layer: Skragg Brown
M Layer

5
Layer: XV-88
S Layer

6
Layer: Flayed One Flesh
S Layer

HORNS

1
Basecoat: Rakarth Flesh
S Base

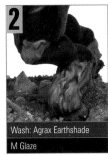

2
Wash: Agrax Earthshade
M Glaze

3
Layer: Karak Stone
S Layer

4
Layer: Ceramite White
S Layer

FUR

1
Basecoat: Zandri Dust
S Base

2
Wash: Agrax Earthshade
M Glaze

3
Layer: Zandri Dust
S Layer

4
Layer: Flayed One Flesh
XS Artificer Layer

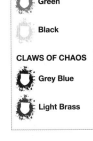

5
Layer: White Scar
XS Artificer Layer

CITADEL PAINT **ON THE APP**

NEW UNIFORM

Want to paint your Chaos Chosen in the colours of another team? Here's a few suggestions.

SKULLS OF KATAM

Green

Black

CLAWS OF CHAOS

Grey Blue

Light Brass

EYES

The Beastman's eyes were painted with a basecoat of Mephiston Red and a small dot highlight of Troll Slayer Orange **(1)**. The Chaos Warrior's eyes were painted with a basecoat of Ceramite White **(2)**. But you could use either style for either player!

1

2

LACES

There are a few ways to paint the laces on your Chaos Warriors (and you might even want to vary them across the team). You can leave them black, paint them to match the leather of the boots, use the Beastman skin stages for a slightly lighter brown or add a bit of contrast with a simple layer of Rakarth Flesh followed by a highlight of White Scar.

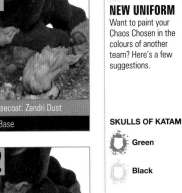

MAY IN BLACK LIBRARY

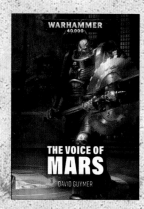

VOICE OF MARS
BY DAVID GUYMER

Charged with unlocking mysterious eldar devices, Iron Father Kristos of the Iron Hands soon realises the xenos are not alone in their attempts to thwart his duty. His own brothers also seek to possess the formidable powers for their own ends. To what lengths will the Iron Father go to secure victory?

HARDBACK | EBOOK | MP3 AUDIOBOOK

WOLFSBANE
BY GUY HALEY

The time has come. Leman Russ, primarch of the Space Wolves, withdraws his Legion from Terra and makes all haste for Horus' position, to try and end the traitor once and for all. But with Horus beyond the touch of mortal blades, the Lord of Winter and War may have doomed himself for the sake of honour…

HARDBACK | EBOOK | MP3 AUDIOBOOK

BLACKSHIELDS: THE RED FIEF
BY JOSH REYNOLDS

Endryd Haar leads his battered warband of renegade Blackshields into battle once more. Answering a distress call from an old friend, Haar seeks out the tithe-world of Duat, intent on plunder. But when he discovers what is hidden there, Haar is faced with a decision that will determine his fate – and perhaps that of Terra itself.

AUDIO CD | MP3

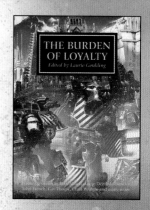

HORUS HERESY JOURNAL

This hardback A5 ruled journal has margin notes that track the timeline of events in the Horus Heresy, making it perfect for fans of the series. **AVAILABLE WHILE STOCKS LAST**

READERS' MODELS

Readers' Models is the place where we share pictures of some of our favourite miniatures painted by you, our readers. Enjoy!

Send your photos to:
TEAM@WHITEDWARF.CO.UK

By submitting photographs of your miniatures, you give Games Workshop permission to feature them in White Dwarf at any time in the future.

Blood Angels Lieutenant
by David Deschenaux

Steelheart's Champions (converted)
by Brendon Jakubowski

Sepulchral Warden
by Thilo Engels

Ironjawz Megaboss
by Julien Doudoux

Dispossessed Runelord
by Laurent Frayard

Death Guard Deathshroud Bodyguard
by Thilo Engels

The Honour Duel
by Michael Azzopardi

Death Guard Lord
of Contagion
by Mateusz Sztraf

Bloab Rotspawned
by Stephan Löppmann

Adeptus Custodes Custodian Guard
by Sam Edmondson

Ultramarines Primaris
Captain in Gravis Armour
by Ben Chatterton

Mortarion, Daemon Primarch of Nurgle
by Thilo Engels

Steelheart's Champions
by Dean Lecoq

Death Guard Chaos Lord in Terminator Armour
by Ólafur Símon Ólafsson

Maggotkin of Nurgle Lord of Plagues
by Christopher Dowson

READER'S MODEL OF THE MONTH

This Primaris Librarian was painted by Riyathe Al-janabi and Yahia Al-janabi. Riyathe tells us more about their joint endeavour.

"My brother and I share an Ultramarines army," says Riyathe, "so we often work on models together. The dark blue armour was achieved by mixing Kantor Blue with White Scar for the highlights and Abaddon Black for the recesses, with an emphasis on contrast to reinforce the shiny look. The cloak was painted Averland Sunset with white mixed in for the highlights and brown for the shading. After we established the highlights and shadows we used a diluted yellow glaze to enhance the saturation. The glow on the Librarian's sword, palm and eyes was done with Ahriman Blue mixed with white and black to get the highlights and shadows."

IN THE SPOTLIGHT: BAS DE RUE

We get sent loads of great photos of painted miniatures every month, but once in a while we receive a selection all painted by one talented hobbyist. This month we look at the work of Bas de Rue.

Bas de Rue has contributed several models to the pages of White Dwarf over the years, including a converted Abaddon the Despoiler back in 2014. Then, he sent us pictures of the models from his Warhammer Age of Sigmar boxed set and we knew we had to feature them. Bas tells us more about his work.

"If there is one style of painting I'm fond of, it's what most people call the classic 'Eavy Metal style from the '90s – the age of Mike McVey with its clean, crisp painting and a lot of contrast. In hindsight, maybe a bit much but, hey, who's complaining? I still look through the painting guides I kept from that era. Being a dad of three little kids, painting is my way to relax and – even if just for an evening – retreat into my own private domain of goblins and wizards. A recent discovery that keeps my mojo strong are the Black Library audiobooks. I listened through the whole of *The Crimson King* by Graham McNeill while painting the Bloodbound shown here. It's just such a great way to immerse yourself in the hobby – I love it!"

1

2

"My favourite model in the set is Vandus Hammerhand **(1)**," says Bas. "His pose is so stalwart and defiant – he reminds me of a classical hero. I took inspiration from the How to Paint Stormcast Eternals book for his colour scheme. I painted his Dracoth Incubi Darkness followed by a layer of Kabalite Green and a wash of Coelia Greenshade. I added a couple of highlights of Kabalite Green mixed with Ushabti Bone, and a wash of Nuln Oil." Bas painted his Lord-Relictor **(2)**, Retributors **(3)** and Liberators **(4)** using the same colours as Vandus.

3

4

"When painting my Stormcast Eternals, I followed Duncan's (from Warhammer TV) advice for painting gold armour – Retributor Armour followed by a Reikland Fleshshade wash gives such a warm and rich golden hue. I just took Duncan's method a step further to make it my own, with washes of Seraphim Sepia and Druchii Violet in the recesses and a few extra highlights of Gehenna's Gold and Runefang Steel to really make them shine."

"Duncan's method for painting the Khorne Bloodbound was a huge help when it came to painting Korghos Khul (5), the Bloodsecrator (6) and my Blood Warriors (7). He taught me a new way to painting Chaos armour – by doing it inside out! You spray the whole model Retributor Armour, then fill in the red panels afterwards. I took that advice from his video on painting Thousand Sons Rubric Marines. To finish my models, I used lumps of tree bark to make rocky bases for them to stand on. I think they help show how inhospitable the Mortal Realms are."

5

6

IN THE SPOTLIGHT
Do you have a collection of Citadel miniatures that you would like to see in the spotlight? Then we would love to hear from you. Why not email us some pictures of your work to team@whitedwarf.co.uk?

7

THE WHITE DWARF GUIDE

New to our games and worlds or just wondering what to explore next? With a huge range of games, miniatures, books and more, there's a lot to choose from. Here's how and where to find out more...

WARHAMMER 40,000

Warhammer 40,000 is a tabletop game for two or more players, where you control an army of Citadel Miniatures representing the Imperium of Mankind or one of its many enemies. Mighty armies clash across war-torn worlds, the bloodthirsty forces of Chaos and myriad alien races striving to overthrow Humanity.

There's big news for Warhammer 40,000 this month as both the Aeldari Harlequins and the Deathwatch get new codexes packed with loads of new rules and background. We also feature an Adeptus Mechanicus army on page 40, while two T'au armies take on two Space Marines forces in a Warhammer 40,000 Battle Report on page 58.

www.warhammer40000.com

FACEBOOK

The Warhammer Community team look after a range of Facebook pages dedicated to our worlds and games. These are pages for everyone, where you can catch up on the latest news, ask questions, show off your own work and chat with other painters, collectors, modellers, gamers and fans. Visit Facebook to find pages for:

f Warhammer 40,000

f Warhammer Age of Sigmar

f White Dwarf

f Black Library

f Forge World

f Blood Bowl

f The Regimental Standard

WARHAMMER AGE OF SIGMAR

Explore the world of fantasy miniatures with Warhammer Age of Sigmar – the game of mighty battles in an age of unending war. Collect and paint vast armies, engage in massed battles and read epic tales of great heroes through an exciting range of miniatures, books and games.

www.malignportents.com

NECROMUNDA

Necromunda is the game of brutal gang warfare in the 41st Millennium. Deep in the underhive of Hive Primus on the polluted nightmare industrial world of Necromunda, rival gangs fight for personal power and the honour of their houses. This month, House Van Saar join the battle for supremacy.

www.necromunda.com

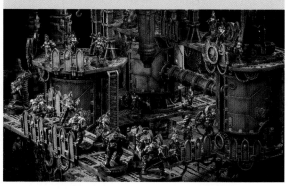

BLOOD BOWL

Blood Bowl is the game of fantasy football. Two players act as coaches, selecting their teams from rosters of Humans, Orcs and the other races of the Old World, taking to the playing field to earn fame, fortune and the adulation of fans along the way!

www.bloodbowl.com

MIDDLE-EARTH
STRATEGY BATTLE GAME

The *Middle-earth* Strategy Battle Game lets you recreate the events of *The Lord of the Rings* and *The Hobbit* motion picture trilogies with your collection of Citadel Miniatures, from the journey of Thorin's Company to the Battle of the Pelennor Fields.

www.games-workshop.com

WARHAMMER UNDERWORLDS
SHADESPIRE

Warhammer Underworlds: Shadespire is a fast-paced game of tactical arena combat for two players, fought out using tailored decks of cards, dice and easy-to-assemble Citadel Miniatures. Build your warband, construct your deck and defeat your rivals.

www.warhammerunderworlds.com

WARHAMMER QUEST

Warhammer Quest is a miniatures game for two to five players. Up to four players take on the role of adventurers, working together to overcome the fiendish obstacles set for them by the master of the Silver Tower or, in the Shadows Over Hammerhal version of the game, the wicked gamesmaster – that is, the fifth player!

THE HORUS HERESY

It is an age of war. Brother fights brother in a hate-fuelled battle to the death as the Imperium itself is torn apart by civil war 10,000 years before the age of Warhammer 40,000. Explore the Horus Heresy with Forge World's range of miniatures and books.

www.forgeworld.co.uk

ForgeWorld

Forge World make highly detailed resin models, large-scale kits and books that explore the worlds of Warhammer 40,000 and Warhammer Age of Sigmar, as well as a range of miniatures for the Blood Bowl, Necromunda and *Middle-earth* games.

www.forgeworld.co.uk

BLACK LIBRARY

Black Library produce novels, audio books, compilations and short stories set in the universes of Warhammer Age of Sigmar, Warhammer 40,000 and the Horus Heresy. You can find Black Library titles in bookstores, our own stores and online.

www.blacklibrary.com

CITADEL

For more than 30 years, Citadel Miniatures have been known around the world as the makers of the finest fantasy miniatures in the world, the centrepieces of Games Workshop's many games and the very heart of our hobby. Check out the whole range online.

www.games-workshop.com

WARHAMMER

Games Workshop stores have been a presence around the world for more than 40 years. Many of our newer and recently refurbished stores are now Warhammer stores, both stocking a huge range of miniatures, games and accessories. Visit your local store for an introduction to our games from our friendly staff.

WARHAMMER COMMUNITY

The home of Warhammer on the web, the Warhammer Community website brings you the latest news on Warhammer 40,000, Warhammer Age of Sigmar, the Horus Heresy, Forge World, Black Library and more!

www.warhammer-community.com

WARHAMMER TV

Warhammer TV brings you regular videos on every aspect of the Warhammer hobby, from daily tips and tutorials on painting Citadel Miniatures to previews of upcoming miniatures and news on the latest new releases.

www.youtube.com/warhammerTV

WARHAMMER LIVE

Warhammer Live is the Warhammer TV live stream where, every month, you'll find over fifty hours of the best live content on Warhammer 40,000 and Warhammer Age of Sigmar, as well as exclusive interviews from behind the scenes.

www.twitch.tv/warhammer

WARHAMMER WORLD

Based at Games Workshop's global HQ in Nottingham, Warhammer World is the centre of the Games Workshop hobby

UPCOMING EVENTS AT WARHAMMER WORLD

MAY

Warhammer Fest

(Ricoh Arena, Coventry)

Saturday 12th – Sunday 13th

JUNE

Warhammer Age of Sigmar: Grand Tournament Heat #3

Saturday 9th – Sunday 10th

Black Library Live

Saturday 16th – Sunday 17th

Warhammer 40,000: Doubles

Saturday 23rd – Sunday 24th

Warhammer Age of Sigmar: Doubles

Saturday 30th June – Sunday 1st July

JULY

Warhammer 40,000: Grand Tournament Heat #3

Saturday 7th – Sunday 8th

Forge World Open Day

Sunday 15th

Warhammer Age of Sigmar: Campaign

Saturday 21st – Sunday 22nd

Warhammer 40,000: Throne of Skulls

Saturday 28th – Sunday 29th

For more information, and to book your tickets, visit our website

Warhammer World, Forge World and Black Library Stores
Buy the entire Games Workshop range from our flagship Warhammer store and the world's only Forge World and Black Library shops.

Exhibition Centre
Explore four halls filled with exquisitely painted miniatures and breathtaking displays from the worlds of Warhammer.

Gaming Hall
Reserve a themed gaming table and do battle with your friends, or join us for an amazing tournament or campaign weekend.

Bugman's Bar and Restaurant
Feast in our Dwarfen tavern, and take home a souvenir from the Bugman's merchandise area.

WEBSITE: WARHAMMERWORLD.GAMES-WORKSHOP.COM   GWWARHAMMERWORLD   TEL: 0115 900 4151
ADDRESS: WARHAMMER WORLD, GAMES WORKSHOP, WILLOW ROAD, LENTON, NOTTINGHAM NG7 2WS

WARHAMMER WORLD

EXCLUSIVE MINIATURES & MERCHANDISE

These and many more exclusive products are available in our Warhammer World and Forge World stores, and at Games Workshop's sales stands at various events.

Joseph Bugman Miniature

Banner Bearer

Eldar Avatar of Khaine T-shirt

Space Marine HQ Command Tanks

Special 30th Anniversary reprint

Realm of Chaos: Slaves to Darkness

Slaves to Darkness Mug

Slaves to Darkness T-shirt

Errant-Questor

Chaos Dwarf Daemonsmith

Elven Union T-shirt

Elven Union Mug

Grak & Crumbleberry, The Right Stuff

THE HORUS HERESY

Space Wolves T-shirt

Word Bearers T-shirt

Legio Custodes Tribune Ixion Hale

Traitor Cataphractii Librarian

Alfrid Lickspittle

Products available subject to stock. All details correct at time of going to press.

IN THE BUNKER

Welcome to the last few pages of the magazine, where we take a regular look at what's been going on inside the White Dwarf bunker over the past month...

What wonders lie in store in the White Dwarf bunker this month? Well, Jonathan and Dan have been trying out the new T'au Codex and both have painted new models for their forces (you can see Jonathan's below and Dan's in the Battle Report on page 58). Martyn has started painting Stormcast Eternals, though he is also still working on the Beastclaw Raiders that he started for our Warhammer Age of Sigmar painting challenge. Mel, Dan and Matt H have also been painting new models for it – we didn't have quite enough space to feature them all, but you can see Dan's Gunhauler to the right and Matt H's latest project on the back page.

WEAPON OF THE MONTH: OCHTAR!
What's got eight limbs, a blade, a cudgel, a pot of ink and a bad attitude? An ochtar, of course! These undersea creatures sometimes act as familiars for Isharann nobles – you can see one floating along behind Lotann, Warden of the Soul Ledgers, keeping hold of his scrolls and quills while protecting him with an armoury of weapons.

MARTYN AND JONATHAN PLAY WARHAMMER 40,000

Martyn and Jonathan have made it their mission to play at least one game against each other every month. Last month it was Warhammer Age of Sigmar, this time around it was Warhammer 40,000. Playing at 50 power in a game of Dark Angels versus T'au, Martyn was dismayed to find that Jonathan had brought a Stormsurge to the battlefield. Even with a unit of Deathwing Terminators able to land behind it, Martyn knew this would be a tough battle. Both players set up units off the board, ready to bring them down where they were most needed. The Stormsurge stood in the middle of Jonathan's deployment zone and dared the Dark Angels to attack.

STATE OF PLAY

Martyn decided to tackle the Stormsurge head on with a unit of teleporting Deathwing Terminators. They inflicted two wounds on the war machine, then attempted (and failed) a charge. The Stormsurge – upgraded with the counterfire defence system and boosted by the point-defence targeting relay stratagem – killed three Terminators with overwatch, then the other two in Jonathan's turn.

Jonathan's Commander flew across the battlefield in his Coldstar Battlesuit and shot Martyn's Chaplain with his fusion blaster. The Chaplain then charged into combat, but was killed by the Commander!

Jonathan's battlesuits armed with fusion blasters caused 16 wounds on Martyn's Predator, obliterating it. One battlesuit died to Aggressors the following turn. Nearby, Martyn's Scouts suffered a painful death at the hands of the flamer-armed Crisis team.

The Dark Angels barely survived to the third turn – it was a major victory for the T'au! The Imperium had much to dwell on.

MORE GUNS FOR BARAK-GLÖM
Dan has continued work on his Kharadron Overlords this month, having finished a Grundstok Gunhauler. His army is now just over 1,000 points in size, though he still wants to add some more battleline units to his force. He's already got an Aether-Khemist and another 10 Arkanauts underway.

REINFORCEMENTS FOR BORK'AN SEPT
As Jonathan mentioned in our Getting Started With T'au article on page 26, he really does like Crisis Battlesuits – this is his second unit, all armed with fusion blasters. "My first unit had flamers for taking on infantry," says Jonathan. "This unit is for dropping down behind enemy lines and killing tanks."

FISH & SHIPS

This month, in a Vox Chatter special, the White Dwarf team discuss their favourite Idoneth undersea creatures (and ships).

Matt H: It's got to be the Ochtar – he's pretty mean looking and he's armed, too. Any model that carries a cudgel has to mean business.

Martyn: I like the buff sea horse – the one on the Eidolon's base. It's so bizarre because it's part horse, part fish, part human – it really gets across the weirdness of the Mortal Realms.

Shaun: I'm going to go a bit bigger and say the deepmare ridden by the Akhelian King. It's like a beast of nightmares, like some kind of undersea dragon-snake.

Michael: The rakerdart on the Soulrender – he looks like an arrow – really fast and deadly, ready to pierce his prey.

Jonathan: On the Eidolon there's a fish with arms – that one! It looks like it's evolving – I reckon it will be holding a sword in no time!

Mel: The clam on the Eidolon's base is awesome – I think it's a great piece for a model's base. It's got a pearl in it, too.

Dan: I really like all the different types of fish on the Gloomtide Shipwreck. Actually, the shipwreck itself is a magnificent scenery piece!

Ben: Allopex. It looks properly vicious and they were really nasty in the Battle Report.

Matt K: You know, team, I'm really not sure this gag has got legs...

IN THE BUNKER

MORATHI, THE SHADOW QUEEN

Last month, we featured Matt H's rendition of Morathi, the High Oracle. Well, after several weeks of intense painting, Matt managed to finish the Shadow Queen version of her, too. "All my Realm of Shadow aelves wear black armour with a red trim," says Matt. "I painted Morathi's scales the same way, reasoning not that she matches them in colour, but rather that they painted their armour to show that they are her servants."

Recently we've had a few people write in asking how Matt paints the skin of his Daughters of Khaine. Well, here's how! He starts with a basecoat of Slaaneshi Grey, followed by a wash of Druchii Violet thinned down with Lahmian Medium. He then applies a layer of Slaaneshi Grey mixed with White Scar followed by a final highlight of White Scar. Matt painted Morathi's wings red to match the ones he painted on the High Oracle version of her last month. ☠